THIS
BOY'S
FAITH

THIS BOY'S FAITH

NOTES FROM A SOUTHERN BAPTIST UPBRINGING

Hamilton Cain

Crown Publishers

New York

Copyright © 2011 by Hamilton Cain

Published in the United States by Crown Publishers, an imprint of the
Crown Publishing Group, a division of Random House, Inc., New York.
www.crownpublishing.com

Crown and the Crown colophon are registered trademarks
of Random House, Inc.

The extract on page 36 is from "I'm No Kin to the Monkey" written by
Dave Hendricks. © 1982 Chestnut Mound Music (BMI). All rights reserved.
International copyright secured. Used by permission. All rights on behalf of
Chestnut Mound Music administered by Cal IV Entertainment, LLC.

Library of Congress Cataloging-in-Publication Data
Cain, Hamilton.
  This boy's faith : notes from a Southern Baptist upbringing/Hamilton Cain.—
1st ed.
    p.   cm.
  1. Cain, Hamilton. 2. Baptists—United States—Biography. I. Title.
BX6495.C24A3 2011
286'.1092—dc22

[B]

2010041026

ISBN 978-0-307-46394-4

Printed in the United States of America

Book design: Ralph L. Fowler / rlfdesign
Jacket design: Nupoor Gordon
Jacket photograph: © Susan Fox/Trevillion Images

10 9 8 7 6 5 4 3 2 1

First Edition

For Owen, Nathaniel, and Peter

*She had gone under a wave, which nobody
else had noticed. You could say anything you
liked about what had happened—but what it
amounted to was going under a wave. She had
gone under and through it and was left with a
cold sheen on her skin, a beating in her ears,
a cavity in her chest, and revolt in her stomach.
It was anarchy she was up against—a devouring
muddle. Sudden holes and impromptu tricks and
radiant vanishing consolations.*

—Alice Munro, "Carried Away"

*It did not give of bird or bush,
Like nothing else in Tennessee.*

—Wallace Stevens, "Anecdote of the Jar"

Contents

Author's Note

The names and characteristics of some individuals
in this book have been changed.

THIS
BOY'S
FAITH

SACRIFICE
OF ISAAC

BROOKLYN, NEW YORK, 2003

Over the course of that cool, damp spring, the news had grown steadily worse. Not long after my wife, Ellen, and I had brought home our first baby, Owen, from the hospital, we noticed he wasn't hitting his early developmental milestones. At two months he couldn't hold up his head. At four months his quick kicks and fluttery hand movements abruptly ceased. His pediatrician described his condition as hypotonic; his muscle tone was acutely low. When she tapped his knee with a rubber hammer, his leg remained inert, indicating the absence of deep tendon reflexes. At her urging, we'd moved numbly through a battery of doctors, tests, and specialists, shuttling from Brooklyn to Manhattan and back to Brooklyn, hoping to pin down the cause of his severe weakness. The conversations were conducted in low, lockjaw tones with sidelong glances—*look how calm and rational I seem, but in reality I'm about to jump out of my skin.*

Then Owen contracted a simple cold, the common currency of infants and children. With no motor neuron ability, he couldn't cough up the mucus that pooled along his airways. As the season turned warmer, his right lung filled with fluid and collapsed. The color in his face faded like a doily, leaving a touch of blue around the mouth. Somehow he knew to concentrate on the next shallow breath, and the next, and the next, the good lung working like a fragile bellows. His tiny abdomen would fist out with a bubble of air, release it, tense again for the inhale.

He lost weight, veering to the point when his tissue would feed on itself, shutting down his organs. The doctors sank deeper into a quandary, debated the pros and cons of a prolonged hospitalization. Snippets drifted back to us.

"We can't seem to get a genetic diagnosis, but we'll call it an SMA phenotype, that's spinal muscular atrophy."

"These patients typically develop chronic pulmonary problems."

"We'll treat him the best we can, but we all must be realistic."

"The statistics paint a bleak picture: most babies with this type of SMA don't live to see their first birthdays, none their second."

Ellen fell into her own depression, weeping in the shower each morning. We braced ourselves for the clinicians' imminent verdict, one that loomed over us like a judge wielding a gavel. *Parents, please rise: just love your child, keep him comfortable until . . .*

And when that sentence stalled before its awful period, when the worst failed to materialize, Ellen rallied. She doled out responsibilities: she'd take care of the 2:00 A.M. feedings

and schedule the copious medical appointments while I'd handle the apartment chores and the frequent runs to the pharmacy. She made lists for the eventuality of a hospital stay,
leaning her willowy frame against the kitchen counter, dark
hair gathered behind horn-rimmed glasses. I'd often give in to
an inner vertigo, however, slumped light-headed for hours on
the couch in the living room and staring out the window at the
ivy-caped wall of the brownstone next door. Stunned into a
stasis, estranged from everything.

"You can't keep it all bottled up," Ellen said. "It will
choke you."

But I couldn't compare it to anything. Except I remembered
flying once, in a commercial jet over Virginia, when a me-
chanical glitch had triggered a sudden, erratic motion. The
pilot had announced that we needed to land ASAP. I'd been
sitting in coach, reading a novel, when the plane lurched to one
side, inscribing a steep, descending arc. For twenty minutes I
bent forward, ears popped, taut body caging a writhing, atavis-
tic snake, while the pilot wrestled us down to an elegant glide
on the tarmac at Dulles.

I recalled what I'd done: I'd prayed. I'd prayed the whole time.

Just an ingrained reflex, or something else?

On Sunday, then, I donned a conservative outfit—starched
shirt with an Eton collar, pressed khakis, and a navy blazer—
and walked the few blocks down Lafayette Avenue, with its
nave of elms, to the imposing brick Presbyterian church. For
a while I lingered on the sidewalk, looking up at the steeple and spandrels, unsure of myself, until a smiling elder,
apple-cheeked and snowy-haired, greeted me with a bulletin
and a handshake.

An image stirred from its dormancy: my father standing in

our church's vestibule in Tennessee, wearing a robin's egg blue leisure suit, handing out bulletins.

Inside, I scanned the sanctuary for some sacred detail to relieve the miasma that had furled over me, heavy as a quilt. The pews' velvet cushions. The green hymnal with gilt lettering blurred from decades of use. The stained-glass rosette window. The spare balcony spangled with red, gold, and azure. Like an emigrant returning to the old country, strutting jauntily down the Jetway into the arms of a thronged family, I felt I'd come home.

Or was the feeling less glorious, more alloyed somehow?

As the organist played an overture, I spied an acquaintance across the aisle, a woman in her late forties, her hair raked into a gray bun, her face waxen. She'd folded her arm loosely around her son, a boy maybe ten years old, saucer-eyed and dimpled, dressed in chinos and a rep tie. Her gesture was so subtle I doubted he realized she was cradling him; yet to me it seemed fierce and protective, evoking a bond I was only beginning to learn, and to mourn.

Another image: another boy, wearing a clip-on tie and sitting rigid next to his mother as she pressed a silver dollar into a brass collection plate.

The choir filed into the loft behind the pulpit, broke into an a cappella song that swelled into a pure, harmonious vibrato. A pulse ticked along my wrist. I felt like an interloper. Did I belong here? The heretic who'd somehow escaped the stake, circling back decades later to sift through the bonfire's ashes, searching for what, exactly?

I bowed my head at the minister's command, hoping to invest the familiar lines with a fresh, raw urgency.

"Our Father, who art in Heaven, hallowed be Thy Name."

Stop torturing yourself. Heretic? Puh-leeez. You did what anyone with half a brain would've: you got the hell out.

"Thy Kingdom come, Thy Will be done, on earth as it is in Heaven."

You know how to do this, you've done this your whole life.

"Give us this day our daily bread."

He's just a baby, you can see his entire rib cage through his skin.

"And forgive us our trespasses as we forgive those who trespass against us."

Shouldn't be this damn hard.

"For Thine is the kingdom and the power . . ."

Feel so useless.

" . . . and the glory forever and ever."

I kept my head bowed long after his breathy *amen,* a sob imprisoned in my chest.

One June afternoon a few weeks later, Ellen and I rushed Owen to the emergency room of our neighborhood hospital. He was suffering from respiratory distress. A nurse whisked him off to the Pediatric Intensive Care Unit, his oxygen saturation dangerously low and his temperature running high.

The pulmonologist listened to Owen's breaths with his stethoscope, commenting darkly on the crackling sounds he heard, the erratic contractions of the baby's belly, the shivering tongue. A surgical team embarked on their own investigation, a spate of chest X-rays and a bronchoscopy, a pygmy camera lowered into the windpipe to check for any anatomical abnormalities—a flap of tissue or a bone spur—that might be constricting the airway. None. The X-rays did reveal an anomaly, though: Owen's collapsed right lung was squeezed like a deflated balloon, his esophagus and heart pressed against its flattened alveoli.

"Ummm, serious," the pulmonologist said, waving a ball-point pen over the images. "Beyond the scope of what we can do for you here." He recommended a move to Columbia Presbyterian, in upper Manhattan. I groaned, already weary of hospitals, jaundiced lights and taciturn doctors, the reek of chemicals and urine, and the cacophony of monitors. A world unto itself, bricked off from the melee of the city but incubating crises of its own.

"Washington Heights, oy gevalt," Ellen said, chin thrust forward, eyes green and hard, twin opals. She hooked a hand along the steel rail of Owen's hospital crib. "At least it's door-to-door on the A train. You know the A runs express, honey, skips the entire Upper West Side?"

"How awesome for us," I said.

"I'll pack those up for you," the pulmonologist said, sliding the films into a manila envelope. "Bear in mind that an X-ray is a two-dimensional image, a snapshot in time, and gives us only a limited amount of information."

A snapshot of a crumpled lung, two-dimensional. Ephemeral as a memory.

As Owen lay in a crib in a special isolation room, a cannula piping oxygen into his nose, I told Ellen I needed my own breath of fresh air. Outside the hospital, I crossed Hicks Street and paced around a playground to soothe my nerves, peering down a sweep of the Brooklyn-Queens Expressway toward the Verrazano-Narrows Bridge, the barbed smudge of New Jersey beyond. My internal compass was pointing south. I fumbled in my jeans pocket for my cell phone, punched my parents' home number in Tennessee. My mother answered the phone brightly—too brightly, given the circumstances. Her melodious drawl kindled images of Chattanooga: the heat-warped docks at Gold Point Marina, catamarans bobbing in Lake Chickamauga's chop, cicadas thrumming in the woods behind the Hillcrest T-ball diamonds.

"Sugar, how on earth are you? Got a little summer cold myself, probably from the air-conditioning. Your daddy likes to crank it up; it feels like Alaska in here! I sure sound like a bullfrog, don't I?" She cackled at her own joke. "Any news about Owen?"

"Things aren't too good, Mom. Ellen and I are going to have to make some tough decisions soon. So I was wondering . . ."

All of my misgivings about my mother flooded into that ellipsis. I mustered the courage for my request.

"We had to admit him here in Brooklyn, and we're transferring him up to Columbia Presbyterian as soon as possible, so the doctors there can help him. I mean, help *us* to help him. He may be there for a long time, maybe months. Is there any way you could fly up for a few days? You could stay at our place while we're at the hospital, feed the cats, clean the bathroom, that sort of thing."

A stilted pause on the line.

"Sugar, that's not possible. Now I *know* you and Ellen are going through a difficult time. Why, we're all praying at church. Gayle Swope just called to ask how Owen was doing."

Gayle Swope: a name I hadn't heard since I was a teenager. Tall, double-chinned, sass-talking Gayle Swope, who, after her deadbeat husband walked out on her, had taken up with my parents and a few other married couples in our congregation. Even in Baptist circles in the 1970s, with divorce a taboo that branded a woman for life, she'd held her head high, putting down roots in her Sunday School class and knitting circle and making nursing home visitations. Across a canyon of years, I saw her at the communal breakfast table at the Glorieta Conference Center in New Mexico, blond hair marcelled like a flapper's, wagging her finger at me in mock reproach. *If your mama won't say it, then I will: don't take such big mouthfuls, there's plenty left for seconds.*

"Mother, it would mean a lot to me. Just to have your support."

A sigh of exasperation, an annoyed tone. "We're praying, Gayle is praying, Jeannie Sanders is praying, we're all praying every night before we go to bed. As your daddy says, prayer is the absolute best way we can support you."

I steadied my voice. "I'm all for prayer, but we could use you, even just to sit with Owen while we catch up on sleep. We're exhausted."

"I cannot just drop everything and run up to New York."

What had I expected from her? All my life I'd heard her self-dramatizing proclamations: *I'd do anything for my family, crawl over burning coals, swim across shark-infested oceans, you name it.* So yes, I guess I'd assumed she and my father would race to my side. To Owen's. In my mind's eye, I saw her with firm jaw, hand on her hip, stepping back steely-eyed into her cone of rationalization. "Your daddy has a follow-up with his dermatologist next week—that appointment was made months ago—and I'm planning to see my doctor as well. My arthritis has been acting up."

I imagined a grim smile tugging the corner of her mouth as

she delivered her coup de grâce. "Why, we're barely well ourselves. We'd only be a burden to you and to Ellen."

My voice cracked. "What about the *next* week?"

Her tone had found its serenity once again. "Sugar, I cannot come to New York anytime soon. That week I'm teaching Vacation Bible School. It would be too late to find a replacement, and all those little children are depending on me."

After we exchanged strained good-byes, I inhaled from the diaphragm, like Owen, to calm myself. Why did I still bring a child's logic to each conversation with her, the magical belief that this time would be different? Of all people, she should be empathetic to my dilemma: she'd lost a baby before I was born.

But those little children were depending on her.

                                                ⌒◦

I hadn't thought about Vacation Bible School in years.

As I was growing up in a devout Southern Baptist household in the 1970s and '80s, church played a central role, especially from the time I was seven, when I came to Jesus on a trampoline. "That Sugar, so eccentric!" my mother would say to Mrs. Swope and Mrs. Norway at Sunday School breakfasts in the Fellowship Hall, nibbling a powdered doughnut and sipping coffee from a thermos she'd brought from home. "Just jumped and bounced his way to the Lord!" The trampoline put a stamp of authenticity on the experience, signaled to my congregation that I was special.

The elders—a few women but mostly men, as only they were permitted to hold leadership positions—considered me a prodigy. Mr. Draper or Mr. Coker would stop my father in the prayer chapel, where the deacons would cluster in their odors of pomade and aftershave. They'd compliment him on his wunderkind: "My oh my, State Winner Perfect in Bible Drill two years in a row. He's going places—he'll be running the entire Southern Baptist Convention one day!" Even our pastor, Brother Roy, whose every word was engraved on the minds and hearts of his flock, had noticed. "Lanny and Cholly," he once said to my parents, "I've got my eye on your boy. That there is somebody."

Each year moved along a worn groove, each season had its set rhythm. Worship service three times a week. Sunday School on Sunday morning, Church Training in the evening, a communal pancake dinner at IHOP with the Cains and the Allisons and Sanderses commandeering the buffet.

In November, an ecumenical Thanksgiving service consisting of houses of faith on the east side of Chattanooga, Methodist and Presbyterian and Church of Christ, the cantor from B'nai Zion, and a pair of stoic nuns from Our Lady of Perpetual Help. Then Christmas, with holly wreaths hung on the sanctuary's portico, bell-jarred candles in each stained-glass window, potted poinsettias tiered beneath the pulpit, their commemorative captions printed in the Sunday bulletin:

This poinsettia given in honor of Mrs. Merilee Draper
From her devoted husband and Martin and Barb

In loving memory of Mrs. Jessie "Nana" Sanders
From her granddaughters Renee, Karen, and Lissy
We miss you each and every day, Nana dear

In honor of Mrs. Cholly Cain
From her adoring husband and children

Trips to Memorial Auditorium to hear Billy Graham or some other evangelist preach "Pay Day Someday," that famous sermon passed down from preacher to preacher like a holy relic. Concerts in the auditorium's well, Pat Boone crooning "Do Lord":

> *Do, Lord, oh, do, Lord, oh, do you remember me?*
> *Look away, beyond the blue* [sotto voce: *horizon*]

Each May the youth group would assume responsibility for all church functions for a week, followed by the frenzy of Revival, with fevered competitions to corral the lost, record numbers of recruits crowding the baptistery. Summer would usher in a recreational slate of activities: barbecue suppers in the Fellowship Hall; day trips out to Lake Chickamauga, with box lunches of baloney sandwiches, Cheetos, and cups of Heinz chocolate pudding. A lifelong sun worshiper, my mother volunteered to chaperone pool events, her attempt to recapture the early years of her marriage, when she'd lived in Florida. To her, tropical weather, water sports, and a golden tan symbolized the good life. She'd slather on the coconut butter, turning ruddy, sprawled in her chaise, archetypal as Cleopatra, while my sister and I would splash around the Cumberland pool, playing Jaws, each of us stroking just beneath the surface with an arm exposed like a fin.

And then there was Vacation Bible School, my mother's personal vacation from *all* parental responsibilities. For two weeks each July, we kids would herd into the musty rooms off the Fellowship Hall, sing "Michael, Row Your Boat Ashore" and "Pass It On," glue Popsicle-stick dioramas of the Crucifixion.

We'd conclude each day with a Bible story, the miracle of the loaves and fishes or the parable of the talents. I preferred the Old Testament tales, the drama and urgency in Genesis. Joseph's coat of many colors. Jacob wrestling with the angel. The Sacrifice of Isaac.

> 22:1 And it came to pass after these things, that God did tempt Abraham, and said unto him, Abraham: and he said, Behold, here I am.
>
> 22:2 And he said, Take now thy son, thine only son Isaac, whom thou lovest, and get thee into the land of Moriah; and offer him there for a burnt offering upon one of the mountains which I will tell thee of . . .
>
> 22:9 And they came to the place which God had told him of; and Abraham built an altar there, and laid the wood in order, and bound Isaac his son, and laid him on the altar upon the wood.
>
> 22:10 And Abraham stretched forth his hand, and took the knife to slay his son.
>
> 22:11 And the angel of the LORD called unto him out of heaven, and said, Abraham, Abraham: and he said, Here am I.
>
> 22:12 And he said, Lay not thine hand upon the lad, neither do thou any thing unto him: for now I know that thou fearest God, seeing thou hast not withheld thy son, thine only son from me.

By Tuesday of the second week, this religious training had grown stale, the indoor gloom like a hospital's, lulled by air conditioners and the recitation of verses. Each cell in my body burned to be outside. My favorite part of Vacation Bible School was the midmorning recess, a respite from the parables and patriarchs. We'd pass around a box of vanilla wafers, toss a plastic football. The church would rent a Winnebago from the local

Coca-Cola bottling plant, park it in the Albemarle Avenue lot, install the gray-haired church secretaries, Mrs. Jarnigan and Mrs. Tomlinson, behind open windows. With six-year-old bravado, we'd swagger up to place our orders.

"What'll you be having today, me laddy?" Mrs. Jarnigan would say, mimicking an Irish bartender. "Coke, Sprite, orange?"

"A suicide," I'd say, ordering the drink of choice at Vacation Bible School.

"One suicide coming right up," she'd say, scooping a plastic cup into the ice bin and rotating it beneath all three fountains. After finishing our suicides, we'd sneak into the playground for "gorilla warfare," a game I'd invented—radio reports I'd heard about the guerrilla warfare in Vietnam and Laos. A dozen six-year-old boys would droop from the jungle gym hoops, making monkey noises and scratching their armpits. On the days when the Coke van failed to appear, we'd swarm across the parking lot in a game of touch football. Once, as a teammate sprinted down an imaginary scrimmage line, I yelled to him to "run like hell." For that infraction I spent the rest of my morning in Mrs. Jarnigan's office and five painful minutes that afternoon with my father's bolo paddle.

Owen's hospitalization stretched into weeks, then months, approaching his first birthday. I kept up the pressure on my parents, and they returned the favor, continuing to resist even after Vacation Bible School ran its course and summer deepened its emeralds along the palisades, across the Hudson River from the hospital. In long-distance conversations, I could hear myself regress to a stammering child, caught swearing in the church parking lot, pleading for mercy.

Ellen and I swapped off shifts, sustained by a flow of visitors, her mother from Los Angeles, her brother from Maryland. Each Sunday my friend Charles and his partner, Konstantin, brought bagels and lox to Columbia Presbyterian, where we'd taken up residence in the Pediatric Intensive Care Unit, or PICU, a spacious, open room framed by thirty curtained alcoves for individual patients, mostly small children and infants. We soon discovered that the PICU resembled a stressed hive, with its low-decibel, everlasting buzz, its hierarchy of drones and worker bees, the attending physician catered to like a persnickety queen. Ellen and I fell into its collective spirit, gleaning bits and pieces about the other cases, pneumonias and muscular dystrophies and liver transplants.

One case in particular troubled the nurses and therapists, a toddler in a crib directly opposite our alcove, something about a marrow disease, possibly fatal. The public nature of the PICU seemed to magnify this child's plight, as though I were staring down the length of a telescope as a tragedy unfolded in slow motion. Day and night a huddle of residents mulled outside his alcove, poring over lab reports, heads cocked in frustration. Barely into their thirties, his parents revolved in and out, ruddy-faced and teary, their movements clenched and robotic as they carried washed linens, bags from Wendy's and McDonald's. Each day I thought the same gut-churning thought: *That could be me, soon.*

Finally, mid-August, my parents acquiesced. My mother refused to fly, citing the terrorist attacks: "No way I'm going to take a plane to New York, not after 9-1-1." They booked themselves onto a five-day seniors' bus tour out of Knoxville.

Since three of those days would be spent on the road—side trips to Jamestown and Williamsburg, the chocolate factory in Hershey, Pennsylvania—they'd grace us with their presence for two whole days.

That first morning they arrived at the hospital, dressed in golf shirts and gabardine slacks. I'd already relieved Ellen, who'd gone home to rest, leaving behind a tote bag of magazines. Since I'd last seen my father at Christmas, his hair had thinned to a silver gauze. My mother had bleached her shoulder-length bob, covering the gray, and when she smiled, a mask of wrinkles erased her eyes. They filed into Owen's room, nodded as I explained the spaghetti of tubes, the gears and whirs of his feeding pump and pulse oximeter machine. A nurse sailed in to check the IV.

My mother gripped my shoulder. "Sugar, all these machines remind me: did I tell you they had to put Shirl-Jo Allison on a respirator?"

"Who?"

"Shirl-Jo Allison, Craig's mother. Last winter. Got pneumonia and they had to take her to the ICU at Erlanger." Her hands danced around her face. "She was okay, but all of us at church were so worried."

"Well, fortunately we haven't had to intubate Owen except for procedures," I said, marveling at her uncanny knack for drawing a line between two disparate points. "He's still not really stable, so the doctors are giving him some supplemental oxygen."

My mother smiled a bland, inscrutable smile. My father had retreated to a lounge chair and was reading *Newsweek*. "This Howard Dean fellow, can't say I cotton too much to him," he said, glancing sternly over the rims of his bifocals. A gaunt, red-eyed resident darted in, looked over Owen's chart, darted out.

"Of course you wouldn't like Howard Dean. He's a Democrat who opposed the war," I said.

"We had to do it," my father said, folding the magazine, nostrils flared, daring me to pick a political argument right here, right now. "That monster was killing his own people."

"Sugar, did I tell you Barb Draper's husband may be called up to I-raq?" my mother said.

"Who?"

"He's in the reserve. Her married name's Gentry. Four children, all girls. You did Bible Drill with her."

My hands curled involuntarily, remembering the spine of a Bible. *Present swords. The Salvation Verse: Begin.* A boy standing at nervous, rapt attention, sweating in an oversize suit and reciting John 3:16, words like sediment in his throat.

I felt a surge of affection when my mother pulled a chair to Owen's bed to read *One Fish Two Fish Red Fish Blue Fish,* e-nun-ci-a-ting the rhyme even though he was really too young for Dr. Seuss. This was her element, entertaining a baby. He watched her intently, craving the cadence of her voice, his unblinking hazel eyes the exact shade of her own.

Ten minutes later she clapped the book shut, stood up, and wiggled her thumb like a hitchhiker, signaling my father.

"Your daddy and I need a cup of decaf. Can you recommend someplace nearby?"

They were gone for almost three hours, returning with a paper bag stained with lukewarm coffee and a bagel smeared with cream cheese. I noticed how far back from Owen's bed they now stood. "*This* is for *you,*" my mother said magnanimously. "You're like a ghost, so white! Bet you don't get outside to work on a tan. And all that weight you've lost, reminds me of, well, did I tell you we ran into Renee Sanders at church a couple of Sundays back?"

"Who?"

"Renee Sanders. Put her on a scale and I bet she don't hit ninety. Never married, although she was engaged once to a high school football coach. Teaches that power cycling."

I looked down at my feet as she prattled on. "Tell you what, Jeannie was thrilled Renee called it off. Said she'd escaped a bullet. I just saw Jeannie last week. We took our friend Ebony to lunch for her birthday."

"Who?"

"Ebony, you don't know her," she said. "She's in my Sunday School class, sings in the choir." She glanced over her shoulder, softened her voice. "She's, um, what do you call it nowadays? Afr . . . Afro-American? My *black* friend, and I love her, I really do!"

"Ebony? Like the magazine?"

"Technically I think she's named something else, but she calls herself Ebony, which is fine with me!"

In the opposite alcove an alarm, one of the unnerving ones, played its screechy xylophone over and over, scattering a gaggle of residents like spooked pigeons. I held a breath a beat, expelled it in a hiss. "We're quite progressive these days," my mother said, grinning, crooking her arms across her chest, a gesture intended to convey she had the upper hand.

I held my palm up, pleading cease-and-desist. She entwined her fingers with mine.

"We were thinking about taking a cab back to Brooklyn. I'll brush the cats. You'll have to tell your daddy which key fits into which lock."

"Fine, but whatever you do, don't disturb Ellen," I said. "She's catching up on sleep."

"Her beauty sleep." She nodded vigorously. "Not that she needs it. She's so attractive, looks just like Barbra Streisand."

"She looks *nothing* like Barbra Streisand," I said, my voice scratchy with fatigue and annoyance. "Just be quiet, okay?"

She nodded again, tapped a finger to her lips. *Shhsssshhh.*

That evening, after the day residents had signed over the PICU to the night crew, I wrestled the lounge chair into a makeshift bed, toeing the footrest forward and tamping down a laundered sheet. I plumped a pillow, fished a paperback novel from my knapsack, flitted from chapter to chapter, distracted. The nurse came in, a ginger-haired waif with an overbite, wrists like a greyhound's shanks. She made a cheery introduction as she rustled up a bedpan and a six-pack of distilled water, a few perfunctory questions about Owen's condition, how long I thought we'd be in the hospital. She whistled as she attended to him, gave him a sponge bath followed by lotions to stave off bedsores. He cooed.

"You love this, don't you, my baby," she said. "Such expressive eyes."

Once she'd stripped and resheeted the crib's mattress, she trundled a scale into the alcove, lifting Owen's flaccid torso into its hammock while I balanced a halo of tubes above his concave chest. His weight had ticked down to 5.2 kilos.

"Not to worry," she said. "He's fighting a deficit—it'll take a few weeks to put on the calories. Then watch out!"

She slipped a cotton gown over his head with one hand, lifting the tubes with her other, tucked him beneath a blanket with the good lung up. He seemed drowsy and content. She teased his armpit with a thermometer—"cool as a cucumber!"—then cuffed his thigh for a blood pressure reading. "Vitals A-OK," she said as she withdrew, pulling the curtain, sealing the alcove into a kind of bathysphere, brutal pressures outside but placid within, the light a cool, watery green. I draped my body across the chair, an ache crimping my shoulders, and closed my eyes, replaying the reel with my parents, thoughts scrolling like jangled glyphs, just in front of my face, a papyrus begging for commentary, some pithy declaration about those long-ago values and how they'd led to this moment.

Sacrifice. An obvious one, woven into the fabric of families like ours. We'd followed cues from the Bible, all those animal sacrifices that bloodied the Temple in Jerusalem. In the intervening centuries, the term had jumped the wispy space from literal to metaphorical, as we sought to carve away our carnal natures for the glory of a higher purpose. Go to church three times a week. Forgo that extra gravy biscuit at the Shoney's breakfast bar. Trade a late-summer idyll at the condo in Sarasota for a mission trip to some off-the-beaten-path hollow in the Alleghenies, where the men would erect a Sheetrock sanctuary while their wives would teach sloe-eyed mountain women how to change diapers, treat lice. Now *that* was sacrifice, the kind that caught God's attention, earned His Love.

But.

But there wasn't much sacrifice to it, really. Instead, there were crass teenagers who mumbled sex jokes when they were supposed to be singing "Amazing Grace." Or the bachelor deacon with the bushy muttonchops, reeking of Aqua Velva, making sheep's eyes at the widows' circle. No appetites renounced on the altar of virtue, at least not in practice.

Steadfastness. The Baptists took this one seriously. To battle Satan's venal schemes, a true believer must always remain steadfast in his faith, constant to the values ordained by the Scriptures, devoted to the Gospel, loyal to spouse and family and tribe. The Bible was rife with examples of steadfast men and women, but one stood out: the patriarch Abraham, whose allegiance to God compelled him to almost kill his own son. If Abraham could pass that test, then we could somehow manage our struggles: flat tires and flash floods, race riots and sibling rivalries, slutty teenagers and babies in peril. We'd handle these challenges with self-deprecating Protestant grace—*shut up and put up,* as my mother would say.

But.

But my mother wasn't exactly the model of quiet tranquillity. Lord, the woman couldn't stop talking—language fueled her like a rocket's thrust. She'd pinball from catty gossip to extravagant praise to biting criticism, often in the same sentence. Years after the fact, she'd still complain about the time I choked in Bible Drill—*you're sagging on those Scripture searches*—or the afternoon my sister dropped her baton in twirling class. Steadfastness was never a simple trait.

Redemption and Apocalypse. The twin nuclei of the Baptist experience, around which we orbited like crazed electrons, banging from one toward the other at supersonic speed. I could tell from recent conversations with my parents that Apocalypse was waxing in importance, as the imagery of the World Trade Center calamity had galvanized the minds and hearts of many south of the Mason-Dixon Line. In the weeks after September 11, 2001, my friend Gittel, Brooklyn born and bred, had encountered evangelical Christians at the site, whole congregations bused in from Texas and Alabama to hand out bottled water and granola bars to firemen and paramedics clawing through the debris field. Potbellies, permed hair, American flag pins on jacket lapels. On the one hand, Gittel noted, they had come north on their own dime, logging sixteen-hour days; on the other hand, they'd asked unwelcome questions about the "peculiar" customs of New Yorkers. *Little lady, them bagels taste like sawdust. Know where I can get a decent sausage biscuit?*

She'd recounted this to Ellen and to me, exasperated, over wine and Brie at our apartment. "Goyishe kop," she'd said, rapping her knuckles on her scalp as if it were a coconut. But it hadn't surprised me a whit. I recognized it as the bifurcated paradox at the heart of growing up Baptist. There were chosen and unchosen, redeemed and damned, clean and not-so-much—nothing gray and ambivalent about that. On the one hand, there were fireballs, shock waves, stick figures plummeting from smoky skyscrapers; on the other, there was the divine reassurance of the Cross, tragedy averted, washed away by a cleansing light. That moment when an angel calls out to Abraham to lower his dagger, Isaac's life spared.

But.

But that transcendent moment was often marred by something more crudely human, like when I was baptized at the age of seven, the dread that had propelled me into the baptismal pool. I'd been a bundle of nerves that day, more focused on the hand of fate than on the pastor's grip as he raised me, snorting, into a transfigured, blessed life.

Magic. The Abraham story illustrated another tenet dear to Baptist hearts: the divine intervention, the serendipitous miracle, deus ex machina. A father confronts his proverbial worst nightmare, the death of his child, but then the Lord tilts the world's axis, the sun sets in the west, a new path forward reveals itself. When faced with possible catastrophe, the Baptists would pray, knowing without a molecule of doubt that the Lord answers prayers. *As your daddy says, prayer is the absolute best way we can support you.*

But.

But sometimes a divine solicitation failed to yield the desired result, like the time I screwed up my answer in Bible Drill, or the afternoon I prayed for the safe return of my kidnapped dentist. This had always bothered me more than it did my fellow congregants, who blithely chalked up unanswered prayers to the opaque mystery of the Lord's Will and moved on to the next thing in a kind of instant amnesia, an almost literary suspension of disbelief. So you petitioned the Lord to boost your chemistry grade but you still failed? No problem! Surely the magic would hold up next time. This sense of the fantastic derived from the Bible, teeming with witches and giants and floods, mutant fish that could swallow a man whole, the lame healed to walk again. Stories that folded back on themselves. Sometimes the Baptists were more Borges than Borges.

A commotion outside. I kicked my sheet to the floor, roused by a wail of alarms. I elbowed the curtain aside, glimpsed the wall clock above the nurses' station. Just past midnight. An incandescence flooded the PICU like stadium lights. I drew the curtain for a full view.

Across the floor, a tableau had staged itself: clumps of nurses and residents, the attending physician in the opposite alcove, pounding on the child's chest. His shoulders pistoned up and down. Above the crib, the monitors displayed parallel flat lines, red os—no pulse, no respiration—a serpentine scrawl beneath, picking up the attending's percussions. The alarms continued to bleep. Someone had pulled the parents away from the crib.

The father, burly in a cotton sweater, brushed his damp face with his fist. "Naw, naw," he yelled, "they said three more months, three more months!" The mother staggered off to the side, bird-boned, a man's oxford shirt baggy on her frail shoulders. My guts knotted themselves. The worst moment of this couple's lives, brutally public, each second chronicled by an unwitting eyewitness, a thirty-eight-year-old man who hadn't shaved in days and couldn't look away.

The attending paused, leaned over with his stethoscope, shook his head. One of the residents nudged him aside, thumped the child's torso, over and over. The CPR had assumed a life of its own, a ghost that cobwebbed the PICU's ceiling. On and on and on. The attending stepped in again. My scalp tingled, mouth dry and oarlike, a tongue of balsa wood. I glanced at Owen. He was sleeping, monitors registering a strong heartbeat, a blood oxygen saturation of 99 percent. I blurted out my gratitude: "Thank God."

The parents milled about outside the alcove, listless, until the attending snapped to attention, peeled off his gloves, and strode over to whisper into the mother's ear. She bolted away from him like a scalded cat, did a weird hopscotch across the floor to collapse outside Owen's alcove, two feet away from me. Her angry yowl: *My baby is dead! I want to hold him! Fuck you, God, you motherfucker, my baby is dead!* Her husband dove forward, seized her ankle, hauled her on her back toward the lobby.

For ten minutes I listened to her curdled fury, her sobs. Then silence.

I reached over the rail to touch Owen's hands, pink and bunched on his chest like starfish. After a while my pulse slowed. I caught my breath, turned around. The nurses had gathered at their station with scrunched brows, glum expressions. A

[23]

priest paced a few feet away, tall and silver-haired and flustered, hand busy at his white collar, mustering his courage before infiltrating the clique of women. A man of faith late to the game, his error compounding the medical failure. They noticed him then. In an instant their dolor transformed into animosity, gushing forward, magmalike, to engulf him. He stepped back to brace himself.

"They told me the wrong floor," he said loudly.

The charge nurse winced. Owen's nurse dropped a can of formula, knelt at the priest's feet to scoop it, looked up through a fringe of ginger bangs. "We sure coulda used you, Father. 'Specially the family."

"They said ER." He drew out the syllables as though to ex-culpate himself somehow, *wro-o-nng floo-uurr, Eeeyy Arrrr.*

The charge nurse shot out from behind the counter like a bullet train, jabbed a finger against the lapel of his coat, her throat quivering its wattles. "The last rites, Father. These were godly folks. The one damned job you're supposed to do, and you screw it up . . ."

The priest rocked back and forth, knees bent, arms scarecrow-limp, a Christian in the pit of the Colosseum, encircled by li-onesses. Life and death, religion and science, men and women; all the intractable conflicts, right there before me, beyond the reach of any pat resolution. He swiveled on his heels, beat a wordless retreat down the corridor, chased by the charge nurse calling after him.

Father, Father.

I drew the curtain shut, crawled stiffly back onto the lounge chair like an octogenarian, wondered again if all those values and concepts I'd learned—sacrifice, steadfastness, redemption, apocalypse, magic—would buoy me when the moment came,

forceful and unannounced, a tsunami breaching the flimsy
dikes I'd thrown up around my life.

The next morning the alcove across the floor gleamed empty,
scrubbed by the housing staff, awaiting its next patient. I'd seen
a similar room a long time ago but couldn't recall it precisely.

My parents arrived to repeat yesterday's routine: a perfunctory hello to Owen, a leisurely interlude at a deli on West 168th
Street. En route to the men's room, I found them sitting in the
lobby and listening admiringly to Ernie, a respiratory therapist
whose loquacious stories peeved the hell out of the rest of the
hospital staff. He was bragging how in a Zen trance he could
lower his heart rate to eight beats per minute.

"For a fact. Docs hooked me up to one of dem pulse-ox
machines."

With arms on the backs of my parents' chairs, I deposited
myself between them, clasping their shoulders for balance, re-
duced to a thirteen-year-old's pose. My mother glanced at me,
her face shining with delight.

"He's telling the most fascinating stories. Never heard of
such a thing." I knew they'd go back to Tennessee with Ernie
as their favorite souvenir, regale their Sunday School class with
a little Yankee show-and-tell.

"You want to come back to Owen's room?" I said.

"Oh, of course, Sugar."

At the baby's bedside, an awkwardness settled over us like a
colorless toxic gas. I recited what the neurologists had told me
about the disease, chapter and verse, the techniques that kept
Owen's lungs clear and dry, my information wilting beneath

a staccato fusillade of *ums* and *uh-huh, Sugar*s. "Well, I know the clock's ticking, but I'm glad you've made such an effort to spend time with your grandchild," I said too loudly. My mother crinkled her eyes, beaming at the false praise, my irony lost on her. She launched into a typical non sequitur. "Did I tell you that your sister is starting her own stationery business?"

My sister, one year younger, both confidante and nemesis. A stream of images: the wisecracking tomboy; the glamorous cheerleader and sorority president; the argumentative lawyer who'd relinquished her practice to embrace a new life as a pastor's wife. Something in her had hardened over the years, as she'd migrated from her breezy, confident-in-her-own-skin youth to a woman jumpy and censorious and high-strung. *Stop talking over me, not that you ever have: you're barking up the wrong tree with embryonic stem cell research.* Oh, yeah, her.

"Kind of like a Tupperware party. She goes to a house and meets with the women and then takes orders, only it's stationery and not Tupperware." My mother wiped a hand against her eyes, voice welling with sentimentality. "Don't know how she does it, running after three little children. Such a brave, brave little woman."

"Can't believe it," I said, shaking my head.

My mother's face tightened into a scowl. "Don't be judgmental."

My father stood, leaned his bulk forward to dam the escalation. He pointed to his watch. "Cholly, time to go."

"You always were a difficult child," she said. "Hardheaded."

"Cholly, time to *go*," my father said.

"Just marched to the beat of your own drummer."

They'd brought their luggage to the hospital, and with an

hour remaining before their bus wheeled southward from the Port Authority, they asked me to flag a cab on Broadway. I could tell they were eager to leave. Without a word to Owen, not even a squeeze of his hand, my mother pivoted, purse under her arm, my father trailing in her wake. As I followed them into the lobby elevator, wobbling with their luggage, I peered into my mother's face, brown as a pecan shell and blasted from all those summers spent at the pool.

"May I ask you a question?" I said, voice betraying an irritation, a desire to spar with her.

"Surely." She picked a fleck of lint from my father's shirt.

"You just left Owen's room without even saying good-bye to him. What's up with that?"

With an eerie, singsong cheerfulness, she said, "Sugar, I don't ever say good-byes, I only say hellos."

As I stood outside the hospital that humid afternoon, staring up Broadway, arm stiff in the air, I tried to see the moment as she saw it. Years ago she'd fulfilled her obligation to me: she'd carted me off to church, schooled me in the Bible's lessons, blending my religious training with my leisure time, ensuring that the church was the hub of all things. Each activity, each thought, each visceral response should spoke out from that hub. She'd given me all the tools I'd ever need. I wasn't going through anything that a little prayer couldn't resolve.

She'd already done her duty. This trip to New York was gravy.

A cab braked along the curb. I gave a thumbs-up to the driver, who popped the trunk. After stowing the luggage, I hugged my father as he sweated lightly, pressed my cheek against my mother's, felt her luxuriate in a task accomplished, something she could cross off her list so she could get back to what remained of her summer.

The car doors slammed, and the cab swung into traffic, fenders filmy with grime. I breathed exhaust as my past sped away from me, only to boomerang back, whipping space and time.

An implacable God tested Abraham's love of Him by demanding the sacrifice of the child of his old age. With Isaac at his side—whippet-thin, clear-eyed, trusting his father's alibi—the patriarch cobbled together a crude altar from hewed stones, shoulders bowed with arthritis and anger at his Deity. He stretched out his son across a bier of dry wood and desiccated vines, head swimming with contradictions, the ardent desire to please God with the impulse to curse Him, both consuming emotions balanced on a blade's edge. As he raised a knife to gore the boy, an angel called out to Abraham, staying his hand: he'd passed the test. He fell across Isaac's contorted body, sapped by the revelation that love and rage could collude together, that a parent's agonizing sacrifice could somehow spare this boy's faith.

What's past is prologue, Shakespeare wrote.

The past is never dead, Faulkner wrote. *It's not even past.*

I

A THIEF IN
THE NIGHT

ONCE UPON A TIME IN CHATTANOOGA . . .

S o do you know why you're here today?"

"Yessir."

"And why is that?"

"So I can tell you how I accepted Jesus."

"Now what does that mean, 'accepted Jesus'?"

"Accepted Jesus into my heart."

"As your personal Lord and Savior?"

"Yessir."

Behind his desk, Brother Roy shifted against the chair's cracked leather, shirt buttons straining against his barrel torso, gray hair greased into a pompadour. His face sagged, jowly, mouth bracketed with commas of wrinkles. The bridge of his horn-rimmed glasses wore a knot of electrical tape. He steepled his fingers beneath his chin, glanced down at a green felt ledger with a copy of the Annie Armstrong missionary budget, a tablet with faint blue lines, a framed head shot of Sister Beryl, his wife, almond brown eyes and a tress of dyed hair.

"Now when did this happen?"

"Sunday afternoon, after church."

"You were at home?"

"No sir."

"He'd gone across the street to bounce on the Twichells' trampoline," my father interjected.

Strange to hear such a transformative event pared down to a simple sentence, but in a sense it was true: home from church last Sunday, I'd stripped off my polyester suit like a dead skin, wriggled into a tank top and nylon shorts, the pair that rode high in my crotch. After a desultory detour past my father's desk in the living room, I'd strolled into the kitchen and silently chewed my lunch, pulled pork on a sesame seed bun with a dollop of coleslaw, then asked my father could I go check out the Twichells' trampoline, which they'd just bought at a sporting goods store on Brainerd Road. My chest was bursting with revelation.

"When the boy come back from the Twichells', he said he was saved."

He was slouching on the divan in Brother Roy's study, beneath a window that looked onto the church parking lot, the Quonset bus garage, and the parsonage opposite it. A dour expression carved lines around his watery blue eyes, his face swollen from sunburn and the snacking-on-Hostess-cupcakes habit he'd recently acquired. The study seemed a capsule cut off from the world, with its shaded lamps, shelves of books, and a curio cabinet brimming with mementos of Brother Roy's travels: bracelets from a Cairo bazaar, polished gems from

Indonesia, a tiny amphora excavated from a cliff near the Dead Sea. Mrs. Tomlinson, his secretary, had drawn the blinds to fend off the afternoon glare, but heat was filtering back through the air-conditioning ducts, dense and stifling.

"A trampoline. Well, that's . . . unusual," Brother Roy said. "Were there any witnesses?"

"Just the dog," I said.

"He was looking after Duchess while the Twichells were up at their cabin for the weekend," my father said.

"Do I know the Twichells?" Brother Roy asked.

"Neighbors across the street, Church of Christ," my father said. "Boys play ball together. I asked him was he sure and he said he was but then I thought it best for him to meet with you so y'all could pray about it."

Brother Roy nodded in my father's direction but kept his gaze fixed on the small, scared orb of my face, his manner pleasant but alert, like a doctor's, humoring me as he probed for a diagnosis.

"Now what does that mean, being saved?"

"Means I'm saved from the fires of hell," I said, swallowing hard. "Don't want to burn in hell. Want to go to Heaven and be with Jesus and my family."

Brother Roy nodded again, as though I'd just confirmed a suspicion. He jotted notes on the tablet, lips pursed. I could hear the scratch of the fountain pen.

"I have a question," he said. "You saw *A Thief in the Night* when we showed it in the Fellowship Hall?"

"Yessir."

"Kinda laid it all out in black and white, yes?"

"It was in color," I said.

"I know that," he said, his voice a frog-in-the-throat rasp
as we approached the critical juncture. "A color movie, absolutely." He coughed into his hand. I could sense something
massive and invisible in the room—God or the Devil, I couldn't
tell which one—but I knew Brother Roy would wrestle it out
of my way, in a feat of theologian's skill.

"How did it make you feel?"

"Frightened."

A Thief in the Night had debuted that spring, sparking prolific
praise from evangelical audiences throughout the country. All
the Baptist churches had rented reels for special screenings. My
parents had granted me permission to kneel at the front of the
darkened Fellowship Hall, head ducked beneath the projector's
ghostly ray as I watched.

Set in the near future, during the prophesied Tribula-
tion, the low-budget film told the story of Patty, a newlywed
who couldn't quite commit to Jesus. She woke one morning
to find her husband, a believer, vanished, leaving behind an
electric shaver on the bathroom sink. From a radio broadcast
she learned that millions of Christians had mysteriously disappeared, all around the globe. Over the course of the film, Patty
fled the militant forces of the Antichrist as they hunted her
down for her refusal to pledge allegiance to their leader. The
film's climactic scene took place at a high dam somewhere in
the Midwest, all canted shots and leering faces. Cornered by
a squadron of helicopters and menaced by a muscular villain
with a goatee and bushy sideburns, Patty scaled a fence, hesitat-
ing a moment before jumping into the whirlpool that sucked
her beneath the floodgate. In the last frame, the whirlpool's
maw rushed up toward her as she fell and fell.

A pang of vertigo doubled me over. God had put this movie in front of me to show me the consequences of a world without faith. Two boys from my Sunday School class, Tad Swope and Craig Allison, had sat cross-legged on the tile floor behind me, editorializing as the story unfolded.

"No, run the other way, the *other way!*"

"Girl, don't open that door!"

"Aw, so stupid."

Tad had leaned forward, rapped me on the shoulder.

"Them 'copters gonna come after you if you don't get saved real quick."

"Bet they got some pretty girls up in Heaven," Craig said. "Like Patty." A giggle betrayed his insincerity.

"Don't you got eyeballs in your head?" Tad said. "Patty ain't going to Heaven. The Antichrist got her. Basically roadkill." He whistled his scorn.

"I didn't say Patty, I said pretty girls *like* Patty," Craig said.

As the credits appeared on-screen, I could hear sobs in the Fellowship Hall, a sense of doom as palpable as the film's dirge-like theme song: *I wish we'd all been ready.*

As the lights came on, I looked around, all those dolorous faces. Something shining and good had withdrawn into hibernation; something meant to be seen plainly, and loved.

"Cholly and I been talking with him for a while," my father now said. "We haven't pushed him." He fumbled for the precise word that would convey his theory. "Well, let's see, guess *A Thief in the Night* made, oh, an *impact.*"

"We got a lot of kids and even teenagers wanting to be saved after we showed that film, Lanny," Brother Roy said to my father. "Our membership rolls have spiked. Seven years old, well—that's young, we usually wait until third or fourth grade to baptize, but he's a smart boy, he gets it."

I'd reached a fork: Brother Roy's road or Patty's. My body closed around this burden and held it in, like diarrhea.

"Did you bring a Bible?" Brother Roy said. "Could you read John 3:16?"

My father pressed his copy into my lap, a King James Version with a supple leather cover and onionskin pages that sighed as I flipped through the Gospels to the somber conversation between Jesus and Nicodemus. My voice quavered, fell beneath the gravity of the moment, fell and fell. *For God so loved the world, that he gave his only begotten Son, that whosoever believeth in him should not perish, but have everlasting life.*

The Salvation Verse, the cornerstone on which the rest of my life would be built. There: I'd read it out loud.

"And this means your name will be written in the Book of Life and forever inscribed, ensuring you a mansion in Heaven, for as Jesus said to His disciples, *'In my Father's House are many mansions. If it were not so, I would have told you.'*"

"Yessir."

"Let us pray then." We bowed our heads. With my lids squeezed shut, I listened to the quicksilver flow of his words, fidgeted until he amened. I opened my eyes. Brother Roy reclined back in his chair, palms down on his desk, grinning at the pleasure of mortaring a new brick into the church's future foundation. My father stood, fleshy and reserved.

"The first in his Sunday School class, my, my!" Brother Roy said. "Leading the pack, as usual. We'll do the baptism this Sunday evening, Lanny. You'll need to show up early, with an extra undershirt and a pair of socks, a change of underwear."

"How about a pair of tube socks?" my father asked. "He has several pair, from T-ball."

"T-ball!" Brother Roy said, capping his pen. "What's the name of your team?"

"The Hornets," I said.

"Plays outfield in the Hillcrest league," my father said. "They name their teams after insects: hornets, wasps, dirt daubers, chiggers."

"The tube socks will work just fine," Brother Roy said. He outlined the procedure: I'd step into the fiberglass well, and after a few words and a full immersion, I'd bob to the opposite stairs and climb, dripping, to the catwalk concealed behind the choir loft. "Five minutes from soup to nuts," he said, a holy parenthesis unlike any other five minutes of my life. He instructed me to cross my arms over my chest and stare straight ahead and not out at the audience.

He rose to show us out, swung open the study's door too vigorously, startling Mrs. Tomlinson as she nibbled a sandwich at her desk. "We'll see you on Sunday, then," he said, lending his callused hand to my father to seal the deal. "Outfielder, huh?"

"Got a big game coming up with the Spiders, week from Saturday," I said.

He punched me on the shoulder. "Good luck, my fine young man."

My father and I descended the stairwell to the parking lot, our footfalls muffled in the building's weekday hush, so removed from the bustle of Sunday or even Wednesday evening, early supper in the Fellowship Hall followed by midweek prayer meeting. The heat had intensified, strangling breath or even a clear thought. My father unlocked the passenger door for me, silent.

We met my mother and my sister at the Red Food store, the anchor of a shopping center close to our neighborhood, shoe-horned in between Highway 58 and a swamp confettied with trash. There wasn't much else on this side of Chattanooga: a smattering of subdivisions, the Hillcrest diamonds, and the mammoth oil tanks of the Colonial refinery.

My mother maneuvered a cart through the produce aisle, listening to my father's account of the interview with Brother Roy. She'd just had her hair frosted at the beauty shop, a platinum sheen over a nest of dark roots. My sister had climbed into the cart's wire-mesh seat, plaid skirt askew, revealing a crescent of cotton panties. She was singing something she'd learned in Children's Church, the cinder-block basement where kindergarteners were segregated during the worship services.

> *I'm no kin to the monkey, no no no,*
> *The monkey's no kin to me, yeah yeah yeah.*
> *I don't know much about his ancestors,*
> *But mine didn't swing from a tree.*

"He brought up that movie," my father said, tossing a couple of tangerines into the cart.

"Don't bruise that fruit," my mother admonished. "You mean that one about the Rapture?"

"Yes, *A Thief in the Night.*"

She halted beside a pyramid of canned niblet corn. "Stay next to your daddy," she said to me. Last month I'd been chasing Derek Twichell around the Red Food store when he'd lost his balance and careened into a tower of canned peaches, gashing his forehead and requiring a few stitches. I leaned back against the cart.

"Did y'all pray, Killer?" she said to my father. In public she usually called him by his proper name, Lanier, or by his ubiquitous nickname, Lanny; but among the four of us, she preferred an abbreviation of his old Army nickname, Lady Killer. The guys in his platoon had christened him when he'd served in the occupation of Germany, just after the war. He'd driven a tank, rising to the rank of first lieutenant before an honorable discharge. Back in Georgia, he'd returned to university on the G.I. Bill, resumed his interrupted business courses, then met my mother. I liked the fact that he had three names, each with its own texture: Killer, with its hint of the macabre; Lanier, like an English duke; Lanny, which morphed into whorls and curlicues when my mother wrote it out in her florid hand.

"Yes," my father said. "Brother Roy said he was young but that he understood."

"Phew, one down, one to go," my mother said. She knelt to embrace me, hazel eyes moist and wide with elation. "Your name has been written in the Book of Life," she said. "You're safe for eternity!" I offered a sheepish grin, flustered by her outburst, her fluttery, female gestures, so contrary to Brother Roy's calm baritone voice as he'd prayed, the stern, masculine business of grace.

At the butcher counter, she inspected cuts of rump meat, ground beef parceled in wrapping paper. "We should celebrate, maybe grill some cheeseburgers," she said. "Or some more of that pulled pork, Sugar, I know you love that. We can ask the Twichells over."

"They're going back to their cabin this weekend," I said.

"They asked you to feed Duchess again?"

"Yessum."

"We'll cook out anyway," my mother said. "To think that just last Sunday you were saved and this Sunday you'll be baptized. The Lord moved quickly—He's got some special things planned for you!"

I believed her. It all seemed preordained.

On Sunday evening, then, I stood at the apex of the baptistery, high up in the sanctuary and just beyond the congregation's line of vision, swathed in an old choir robe and a blue satin collar, a T-shirt and shorts underneath. I stepped into the water, warmer than a bath, not tepid as I'd assumed. It rose to my shoulders, gave off a whiff of chlorine. The custodian had dimmed the sanctuary's immense chandelier, keeping the footlights on in case of an emergency. A floodlamp beamed down into the pool, scattering light.

I came sluggishly into view, the robe's folds billowing across the surface. Brother Roy had positioned himself in the waist-deep middle. Below his robe he was wearing rubber boots, the kind I'd seen my father use on fishing expeditions on Lake Chickamauga. The pastor put his arm around me and prayed aloud, funneling his words into a microphone mounted on the baptistery's glass wall. I felt a handkerchief over my nose, my knees loosening to jelly as he dipped me.

"I now baptize you, my little brother, in the name of the Father, the Son, and the Holy Ghost."

Held down for a moment, I thrashed, a child's involuntary protest, saw him prismed over me until I broke the surface and breathed again. He wiped my eyes and hair with the soggy cloth, his voice brogued with feeling. "Raised to walk in a newness of life."

He released me. As I mounted the stairs on the opposite side,

I felt my bare toes and looked back. One of my tube socks had peeled off and was now floating portentously in my wake, the red and black colors of the Hornets blotching the purity of the space. Brother Roy hitched his robe to snag it, a serene, fluent motion.

I was now officially a Baptist Boy, like those boys before me who'd been dunked in fiberglass tanks and swimming pools and cisterns and even in the muddy, serpentine rivers that veined the South, all those unscrupulous male souls flayed and then bleached to an immaculate gleam. A fraternity cemented in deacons' breakfasts in the Fellowship Hall, when a guest speaker, invariably a dough-faced former University of Tennessee outfielder or an aging all-American linebacker from Georgia Tech, would bless the Krispy Kremes and then confess how Jesus had washed away the stain of his wayward sports-hero youth, those keggers and that drunken whoring. All these men had started out just like this: with a prayer and a plunge. My older cousins, some graduated from seminary in Louisville and shepherding their own congregations in Georgia and South Carolina. Church elders like Mr. Sanders and Mr. Welch and Mr. Draper, paragons of virtue. Brother Roy. My father, who now greeted me at the top of the stairs and escorted me into a closet back behind the organ pipes, where he toweled me off, helped me into a change of clothes, arranged each lick of damp hair with his tortoiseshell comb.

Afterward he accompanied me downstairs to the reception in the Fellowship Hall, where my mother and sister waited for me, cups of ginger ale in hand. Mrs. Swope paced the room with a plate of gingersnaps and butter mints. My mother had worn her best sleeveless dress, gingham daisies embroidered along the neckline. She tossed a slender arm around me like a lariat, talking a mile a minute, her euphoria calming the shudders she couldn't see. My parents' friends—the Welches and Sanderses and Allisons—mobbed me.

"Thank you so very much, Shirl-Jo," my mother said. "Bet it'll be Craig's turn next."

Mrs. Allison tipped her head back in full cackle. "If the Good Lord don't save Craig soon," she said, "the Devil's gonna snatch him up!"

Their tasks performed, Brother Roy and my father had drifted into a conversation about SEC football, that Heisman prospect recruited by Bear Bryant. I glanced over at the far wall. Craig and Tad and Trudie Parham had whipped out their yo-yos and were doing Walk the Dog and the Swing, pretending to ignore me as I preened in the warm spotlight of adult approval. I knew they were jealous that I'd been the first. But they couldn't grasp that I needed to be saved from something more immediate than the acid lakes of hell, the thing that was scalding me inside.

When the boy come back from the Twichells', he said he was saved.

Something else had snared me in its dragnet that previous steamy Sunday, spurred me across the street and into the Twichells' backyard.

Home from church, I had yanked off the clip-on tie and slung away the leisure suit jacket, unbuttoned the polyester shirt. Through my window I could see a shimmer off the Twichells' driveway, across the street. I left the pants upright in the middle of the floor, listing like a tent; stood in my briefs and sock feet, abdomen distended with the gravy biscuits I'd devoured before Sunday School. I rummaged through my bureau, fished out the nylon racer shorts and tank top with the H. R. Pufnstuf decal, and pulled them on. Away for the weekend, up at their lake property on Watts Bar, the Twichells had asked me to feed Duchess, their brindle bulldog.

"Sugar, lunch," my mother yelled down the hall.

"Too hot to eat," I called back.

"That's just too darn bad, seeing as how I've already fixed you a sandwich."

I found her in the living room in a mood, bent over my father's desk and rifling through a bundle of envelopes. She'd tipped over the praying hands sculpture. "Where's the mortgage?" she muttered to herself. "Killer, I swanny." She was wearing just a bra and slip, hair piled on her head and shedding bobby pins, an intermediate stage between the high-waisted paisley dress she'd worn to church and the bikini she'd lounge in until four, four-thirty, when she'd shower for the evening service. In frustration she slammed the drawer shut, but it jammed open.

"Ain't hungry," I said.

"The last of that pulled pork from Renner's Smokehouse," she said, glaring at me and nodding toward the kitchen. "Scraped the bottom of that carton myself. And don't say 'ain't.'" She stamped down the hall to search the metal deposit box my father had squirreled away in his closet.

I righted the sculpture and nudged the drawer in gently, but it hooked on a translucent plastic pouch. I tugged the pouch loose, spilling my father's old Army photographs, glossy and scalloped along the edges. Familiar images I'd seen numerous times. A cathedral, an arched bridge over a river. Candids of his buddies posed in front of a jeep, mugging for the camera, lean and shirtless and dog-tagged. My father in his fatigues, choir-boy young and splayed out in a drift of snow. Another one of him in a tank's turret, crew-cut hair and a gap-toothed grin, hand caressing the cannon's muzzle.

At the back of the cache was the most alluring photograph of all: a tinted studio portrait of a woman in three-quarters profile, a dark braid coiled above her forehead and a plush gown off the shoulders, a hint of cleavage fading into a note penned uphill in a block script. *Larry, remember that you'll always be mine, Ruth.* The *r*'s in the man's name hooked over, almost like *n*'s. Larry, Lanny: the spelling suspiciously close, reminding me of the way my mother would embellish my father's nickname in her ornate cursive. When I'd asked my mother about Ruth, she'd laughed, claimed that the picture had belonged to another G.I. named Larry, whose gear had gotten mixed up with my father's when they'd shipped back to the States.

I tucked the pictures back into the pouch and then noticed a manila envelope wedged along the drawer's roller, something I hadn't seen before. I wrenched it loose. Inside was a yellowed mimeograph form. I scanned the heading.

UNITED STATES ARMY
APPLICATION FOR MARRIAGE LICENSE

DATE OF APPLICATION: January 18, 1951

APPLICANT'S NAME: Lanier "Lanny" Cain, Gainesville, Georgia, U.S.A.

COAPPLICANT'S NAME: Ruth von Hoeffler, Ulm, Baden-Württemberg, Federal Republic of Germany

I looked away, inserted the form back into the envelope, and placed it at the bottom of the drawer, weighted down by the photographs. I shut the drawer and held my breath for a moment, dizzy with my own pulse, a door rhythmically banging open and shut in some exhausted, war-charred land.

In the kitchen, my sister was sitting in her booster chair, engaging a pair of Barbies in a stiff-armed catfight along the table's drop leaf. She'd pushed away the grilled cheese sandwich my mother had sliced along the diagonal. I slouched into my chair in front of my paper plate, chewed each bite of pork thoughtfully. My father hunkered over the counter, T-shirt bunched along the elastic band of his Bermuda shorts, dangling a canister of Cheez Whiz over a tray of Ritz crackers, decorating each one with the concentration of a pastry chef.

"Want some crackers?" he said without glancing up.

"Okay."

He brought the tray over, and I popped one into my mouth, felt it dissolve into sawdust.

"Can I go feed Duchess now?" I said.

Something in my voice caught his attention. He swam out of the stream of his thoughts to regard me. "You want to bounce on that trampoline the Twichells got at Murphy's."

"Derek said I could."

"Didn't you feed Duchess last night? The Twichells should be back in a couple of hours."

I spelled it out: "Derek *said* I could *bounce* on the trampo*line* while they're *gone*."

"Fine then."

I dashed down the stairs and through the garage, past the station wagon and Pontiac drizzling their oils, an odor of exhaust. Across the street, I bypassed the Twichells' front walk for the flagstone path that meandered toward the backyard, where I flipped open the chain-link gate and slipped inside. The bulldog lumbered out from her shadowed lair beneath the redwood deck, past a tin pan of last night's rainwater and a rusted colander of Alpo, half-eaten. Panting, she thrust her blunt snout into my hand.

"Got nothing for you, girl," I said.

She withdrew into a nimbus of flies and waddled off into the tall grass, squatted to relieve herself. I swung onto the trampoline and locked my knees, testing the flex and give of the taut fabric. For a while I mimicked the jumps I'd practiced in the deep end of the Cumberland pool, the cannonball and jackknife and scrambled egg. Rhythmic belly flops, a full-body slam, until the momentum died away and left me inert and curled like a shrimp, staring up at a weave of live oak branches, a bowl of pewter sky. I smelled the slow approach of storms.

You'll always be mine.

What if she tried to steal him away, like a thief in the night? It was up to me to convince God to not let that happen. I'd strive so hard to be good, Mr. Perfect from here on out, all the way to Heaven. I'd save myself, my family.

I stood and lunged vertically like a pogo stick, kicking my feet outward for more lift, inching the plane of trajectory higher. The springs complained with my weight. I achieved apogee with arms flung into a cross, each cell kindled by a flare of feeling. From the peak of my jump, I could see past the Twichells' fenced yard and across the street and past my own frame house to a thicket of sweet gums that marked the neighborhood's boundary; beyond, a field dismal with weeds, and the silver domes of the Colonial oil refinery, a half mile away.

A brilliance itched beneath my skin as the universe played out its intricate physical laws inside this seven-year-old boy, hurtling his arc farther and farther up, ascend and ascend.

A stutter in the springs. I toppled forward, fell and fell.

I am still falling.

I pitched onto the trampoline's far side, managing to stay on. The world wobbled into its set lines: the overhang of the redwood deck, a screen door resined with insects. A rumble from the north, toward Lake Chickamauga. I vaulted into the grass, face flushed from an incandescence I hadn't known existed until now. The bulldog raised her head to contemplate me and then bowed again, prayerlike, rooting for scraps left over from the Twichells' last barbecue.

I eased back through the gate and down the flagstone path, looked both ways before I crossed the street as my father had taught me to do, dragged my feeble shadow across my own front yard.

Ruth had swooped into my life, a malevolent angel with a cruel smile, body voluptuous in a tunic, eyes spaced wide and pupil-less, a statue's. An ocean meant nothing to her. Now she'd embedded herself in the ball of my skull, where she preyed like a Venus flytrap on the thoughts that buzzed there, her leaves hinged open, waiting to spring.

As the excitement over my baptism ebbed, I fretted about Saturday's T-ball game. The Spiders sat enthroned at the top of the Hillcrest league. An upset would catapult the Hornets into the lead for the pennant. As the smallest player in the entire

league, I'd been strategically placed at the bottom of the pecking order: outfielder and dead last on the batting docket. Few
grounders dribbled past the infield, and I could cycle in and
out of my turn at bat with a pop fly inevitably picked off by the
shortstop.

A few innings into the game, I could see that we had a
fighting chance. The Spiders were down a couple of their star
players, thanks to a weird summer flu, so the score had swung
back and forth until the top of the ninth. The bill of his cap
pulled down, my father called the plays at third base, while Mr.
Twichell crouched behind home plate in an umpire's uniform
and mask, inserting the ball into the rubber cup in a show-offy,
exaggerated manner, as though he were crowning a sundae
with a maraschino cherry.

Exiled to my usual outpost—right field, away from the
fray—I found a pine twig and used it like a pencil to etch a
name in the dust: *Ulm.* With the toe of my cleat, I erased the
m's second hump, scratched a line above the first hump and
crossed the *l,* added a capital letter to the new word. *RUth.*

Larry, you'll always be mine.

I glanced at the bleachers, where my mother frowned in
the top row, a red-checked kerchief looped beneath her chin,
her arm around my sister. There were mostly women in the
bleachers, the raven-haired Mrs. Twichell and some other
Hornets mothers I recognized but some unfamiliar faces as
well. What if Ruth had flown on a jet from Germany and was
now sitting there, wearing sunglasses and a wig as a disguise?
I imagined her waiting until the end of the game, when she
could claim what she felt was hers, saunter unnoticed behind
third base and with a crooked smile and a flash of her blue

eyes seize my father's arm, spirit him back to Ulm, back to a chalet where a grown daughter and son pined for him, blond and lantern-jawed . . .

A ball skittered past me, spitting dust. I heard my father shout, "Don't just stand there." From the bleachers, my mother's voice, irritated, "This ain't a hootenanny, Sugar, get in the game." I chased the ball down and ladled it into my bulky glove, threw it overhand to the pitcher. No matter: the Spiders took the lead again.

A few minutes later we jogged into the dugout for the bottom of the ninth. I sat down on the bench next to Derek Twichell, a blubbery, fair-skinned boy a year older, hair coarse like straw.

He grimaced at me. "Shoot, can't believe you screwed up. Them is gonna win for sure. You suck donkey dicks."

"Shut up, Derek," I said.

"You shut up, Piglet, or I'll squash you like a bug," he said.

The first two players up, the cream of our team, swaggered to the tee, obligingly sent balls straight into the glove of the Spiders' pitcher. It looked like the whole thing was over. Then Derek ambled to the plate, sweated and grunted as his father teed the ball, let loose with one of those new aluminum bats. The ball rocketed through left field, the Spiders' blind spot, pinged the scoreboard, and bounced back into a patch of clover. Any other kid would have run the bases lickety-split, loped theatrically into home to slap the hands of his teammates, but Derek, huffing, was lucky to reach second, where he swanned around in a haze of self-congratulation, bowing to cheers from the bleachers. He kept bowing after the play was over and Mr. Twichell had once again teed the ball.

From the dregs of the batting docket, I stepped forward, the player my teammates sneeringly called Runt and Piglet, aluminum bat bearing down on the knob of my shoulder. The whole infield was on high alert. I plotted the invisible line around the diamond: no linear path to transcendence for me but rather one that zigged and zagged back to the point where I now stood in a blur of gnats. In one faltering movement, I *thwacked* the ball. It hugged the smooth curve of Derek's hit through that chink in left field and toward the chain-link fence. Both the shortstop and the second baseman leapt into the air, groaned as the ball whizzed between them.

A pause. I could feel her breath on my ear.

I heaved the bat and sprinted to first base. Veered left toward second, which I stabbed with my right cleat, pushed through a cloud of orange dust toward third. My father loomed up from the chalk-marked coach's box, red-faced, arms thick as hams, voice cracking with fury. "Go back!"

I stared up at him, terrified.

Larry, remember you'll always be mine.

He's known as Lanny or Killer. Not Larry. There's no such man.

"Back to first base," he screamed. "Do as I say!"

I pivoted and retraced my steps, dodging a commotion at second—something seemed to be going on there—and ran back to first, tagged it with my cleat, heard my father's piercing voice across the diamond, "Now go to second!"

I sprinted to second and halted there, breathing hard. The Spiders' pitcher barricaded the way forward, clutching the ball in his glove. Beyond him my father was still in his coach's box at third base, deflated. Mr. Twichell swept his hands horizontally. "Safe!"

Safe for eternity.

I'd never hit a double before. The Spiders' coach emerged from their dugout. At home plate he leaned in to whisper to Mr. Twichell, the panorama of the infield reflected in his aviator sunglasses. "Naw, naw," Mr. Twichell said, agitated. The coach whispered again. An uneasy pause.

"Son," Mr. Twichell yelled to me, "I'm afraid to say you're out."

Out—the opposite of safe.

A titter of dismay from the bleachers. My mother wagged her finger at my father. In his triumph, Derek had tuned out the possibility that I might actually succeed in knocking the ball into the outfield, just as he'd done. He was blissfully unaware when I ran past him and toward third, which explained why my father had insisted I backtrack to first base; he was hoping to coax Derek toward third, with both of us scoring runs to win the game. Instead, as the Spiders' coach pointed out, the rules manual was clear: by lapping my own team member, I was technically out, and the game over. We'd lost. Both teams lined up at home plate, touched gloves. The Twichells hung back, ostensibly to collect the bats, but I detected a chill between my parents and our neighbors.

In the station wagon, my mother yammered on about how unfair it all was, how Derek had stolen my chance at T-ball immortality. "That tub of lard," she said. "Can't figure out why Chip and Mary Jane don't put him on a diet. Every time I see him he's eating some hot dog or Creamsicle." Kerchief disheveled, she twisted around in the front seat to study me. "Killer, Sugar's upset," she said to my father. "I firmly believe he may very well be traumatized."

Larry, remember . . .

But there's no such man.

"Guess I messed up," I said.

"Messed up? You?" my mother said, incredulous. "It was *Derek Twichell* who done you wrong. Always off in the twilight zone, that lard butt. In other words, it's not your fault. I may very well call Mary Jane and tell her what I think."

"You'll do no such thing," my father said. "I can swing by Hardee's if the boy wants."

"Some consolation prize," my mother said.

I knew then that they'd discourage Little League next year—knew and didn't care. I'd shucked off the carapace of earthly concerns, its competitive ball games and low-budget propaganda movies and mysterious women in vintage photographs, bounced and jumped my way toward an exalted plane, light as ether. The afternoon had ground down into dusk and disappointment, but I honestly felt unaffected, detached, a sensation that persisted after the cheeseburgers and milk shakes, my parents retiring into their bedroom across the hall to watch the Carol Burnett variety hour.

After I said my prayers, I flicked off the overhead light and stretched across my upper bunk, arm drooping over the side. I felt just that much closer to God. He'd saved me from Derek's jeers, from those kids at church who scorned my pious ways, from the gargoyle in my head, her lips wet, curled in a snarl. With eyes half-shut, I consigned that other boy, the one from two Sundays ago who'd raced across the street to the Twichells' trampoline, to the lower bunk forever. I could see him now for who he was: unredeemed, lesser. On the surface my identical twin—same scrawny torso, spray of freckles across the nose, a light brown widow's peak—but with a soul brittle and remote, cold and sterile as a gibbous moon.

The roar and tremors threw me awake, an earthquake detonating beneath the house's foundations. I fell and fell.

I hit the floor in a tangle of blankets. A *pfffsst,* like helium escaping from a balloon. The room drenched in an orange light, bunk bed tilted against the wall. I rolled into a stoop and stood, a move I'd learned in tumbling class.

"Oh, my God," my mother shouted from across the hall, profaning the Lord's Name in her fright.

"Power's out," my father said groggily. "Just tried the light switch."

I paused outside their bedroom door. My mother swayed in silhouette before me, a bundle against her shoulders. My sister, still asleep. The light brighter now, like a thousand candelabras. Waves of heat rattling the windows. "We got to evacuate," my father said, peering out.

"Killer, what is it?" my mother said.

"Oil refinery. One of those tanks exploded."

There was no time to dress. In my pajamas, I padded after my parents down the stairs and through the basement and into the garage. As my father jimmied open the garage's door, my mother stowed us in the station wagon's hatch, my sister yawning awake. We drove down back streets toward Highway 58. The power outage had spread, snuffing out streetlights. A rich glow suffused the neighborhood. Other families slunk onto sidewalks and into carports; one girl wrestled a leashed Saint Bernard into a Volkswagen. Soon a caravan of vehicles wended in a ragtag line toward the Red Food store, honking their horns.

We circled the parking lot until my father angled the car into a slot on the far side, next to the swamp. Another engine idled next to us: the Twichells' van. My mother rolled down her window as Mr. Twichell leaned out, the tension of yesterday dissolved in a common purpose.

"Y'all come take refuge with us," he shouted over a blare of sirens.

Mrs. Twichell slid open the side door, and we climbed into the van, woozy with fear. My mother and sister clambered past Derek and his two-year-old sister onto the jump seat while my father and I huddled in the rear with Duchess and her slobbery grunts. Coronas of flame boiled up from the refinery a couple of miles away, smoke smudging a darker ink against the night sky. The ground thundered again, a spasm of fire that illuminated a deck of clouds.

"Another one gone," my father said.

"Bet we make Walter Cronkite tomorrow," Mr. Twichell said.

No one said anything more as we lapsed into a fugue, unable to drive farther away, across Chickamauga Dam or toward downtown. The fire swirled higher into the sky, two hundred, three hundred feet, as another tank blew, and then another. My father yoked his arm around my waist, his hand seeking my hair as if to reassure himself that I was scared but okay.

Safe for eternity.

For a long while I slumped against him in a wash of ocher light, queasy, like I'd felt on the trampoline. A hammer crashed in his chest. Years ago he'd buried the story of Ruth, whatever she'd meant to him, traded gold rings with my mother, slipped innocuously into a life of routine—a Monday through Friday job, weekend prayer breakfasts, shut-in visitations—always smiling as he chatted with his fellow deacons each Sunday morning outside the sanctuary, verses of Scripture blended with current SEC stats, who was in the running for this year's Heisman Trophy.

A stink of gasoline leaked into the Twichells' van. He tightened his grip.

These deceptions, of course, will endure past this moment, long after firefighters have extinguished the blaze, assuming a complexion as singular as a lover's eye, as intimate as the smell a wife leaves behind in the shower. They'll grow in heft, from casual beginnings—sweet nothings men and women whisper in bed; the fibs a mother lavishes on a child to perk up his mood when he strikes out at home plate—to deeper, more serious lies, lies uttered in anguish and disbelief, a mantra a father chants at his child's bedside in a hospital a thousand miles away.

You'll always be mine. Safe for eternity.

Saved.

2

J. C. PURGATORY

One afternoon the week before Christmas, my father hunched behind his desk in his cubicle office on the second floor of JCPenney, the flagship retail store at Eastgate Mall. The PA system crooned a Muzak rendition of "Deck the Halls." On the floor below, crowds clogged Men's Suits and Home Appliances, swarmed the Young Misses' department and the costume jewelry counter: all encouraging signs of a robust season. His telephone rang as he snapped a rubber band around a sheaf of receipts. He tucked the receiver between his chin and shoulder, a cuff-linked wrist astride the paperweight on the desk's surface, a toddler's sneaker bronzed and mounted on a marble shingle, its toe tamping down a metal plate etched with a double monogram: *H.H.C. & C.C.* Beneath the plate he'd taped an admonition: *Not to Be Used as Ashtray.*

Seconds later he was dashing down the back stairs to Toys, perspiration clammy along his forearms. A couple of policemen intercepted him, their belt radios blatting staticky voices.

That night he summoned my sister and me into the living room. My mother sagged against him on the green velvet love seat, face haggard, hands writhing in her lap like eels. My

father led us in a prayer for the five-year-old girl who'd disappeared while her mother harangued a clerk over the price of
an Easy-Bake Oven. The woman had turned to see a gap in
the aisle, let out a scream. A lockdown of the whole store had
produced only a mitten. A couple of customers claimed they'd
seen a man holding a child's hand, hustling her toward the
parking lot.

I associated Penney's with violence. Some months earlier,
at closing time, a man had tried to rob the till in the Sporting
Goods Department, knocking over a pyramid of basketballs as
he dove for the open drawer. An assistant manager had pinned
him down until the perp pulled a switchblade; after slicing the
assistant manager's hands, he'd run off toward the store's entrance, by the beauty shop, where he was tackled by a security
guard. He'd bucked as the cuffs clicked around his wrists, shattering a glass door. In the middle of the night, we'd all ridden
with my father down to the store, where under his watchful
eye a janitor had swept up the shards and swabbed the aisles,
blood mapping out a frenzied story, each pink splotch an exclamation point of panic.

In a quavering voice, my father now asked the Lord for the
girl's prompt return by Christmas, said amen. My sister and
I rocked on our bare feet, flannel pajamas belled around the
shins. This was how the world worked: we prayed and the Lord
would heed.

If a child went missing or fell from a jungle gym, if we did
something bad, like shoplift sour balls from the candy counter at Murphy's, we could withdraw to a bathroom, shut our
eyes, and beseech forgiveness. We did not need a priest for that
rush of relief and sanctity. We did not need the Virgin for that
twinge in the abdomen. The Lord saw us as being as essential

as his own Mother, knew us to be equals of Peter or Priscilla or Paul, those figures we'd glimpsed in the encyclopedia, their marmoreal robes gracing the airy transepts and barred-off chapels of cathedrals, whose chiseled likenesses entombed the Holy Spirit like a genie in a bottle. In another world, the Virgin might bring a sinner closer to God, her lithe hand shepherding a child toward a hazy incandescence, but not in ours.

The saints might suffice for others, but not for us. God lived in the cathedrals of our hearts.

For almost a week Chattanooga cowered on its knees, praying, praying: the hyperventilating Baptists and the reserved Methodists swarming sanctuaries; starched-shirt Presbyterians and country-club Episcopalians bobbing their chins, their puny numbers confirming their elitism; a smattering of Catholic families flocking to Our Lady of Perpetual Help to mutter Rosaries for the missing girl. A city moved its lips in prayer, and the Lord heard. On Christmas Eve, a drifter carried the child, swaddled in a quilt, into a mall in Atlanta and dumped her at a Penney's there. In a deposition, the girl's captor said he'd contemplated hurting her—beating her, raping her, or worse—but a voice in his head had commanded him to refrain. The power of prayer, Mr. Sanders whispered to my father in the church vestibule.

In the week between Christmas and New Year's, I went with my mother to Penney's for the holiday markdown sales. She reconnoitered the aisles, a firm grip on my shoulder, seeking out discounted wrapping paper and ceramic Santa Claus mugs, a jumper for my sister or a pair of loafers for me. From beneath her arm, I watched a gaggle of nuns as they scavenged the bargain racks for worsted-wool coats, out of fashion but

voluminous enough to cover their habits, the dark fabric a for-
malist rebuke to our emotional, freewheeling ways.

In mid-March, the jet stream plowed down from Canada at
the exact moment a well of low pressure deepened into a cyclone over the Gulf of Mexico. The gulf's temperature was too
cool to fuel a hurricane, but the storm still caused damage as it
whipped across Alabama and Georgia, drowning culverts and
shredding power lines, spinning top-crazy over Chattanooga,
gorging Friar's Branch and Chickamauga Creek and the Tennessee River.

I recalled the story from Genesis:

7:11 In the six hundredth year of Noah's life, in the second month,
the seventeenth day of the month, the same day were all the fountains of the great deep broken up, and the windows of heaven were
opened.

7:17 And the flood was forty days upon the earth; and the waters
increased, and bare up the ark, and it was lift up above the earth.

7:18 And the waters prevailed, and were increased greatly upon the
earth; and the ark went upon the face of the waters.

7:19 And the waters prevailed exceedingly upon the earth; and all
the high hills, that were under the whole heaven, were covered.

"Got a ways to go before we make Noah's flood," my father
said one morning as he twiddled the dial of the clock radio
on the dresser. The local AM disc jockey was rattling off a
list of school cancellations: Central, Howard, Girls Preparatory

School, Signal Mountain Elementary. The Christian academies were closed. The entire Eastgate Mall, from Miller Brothers to Loveman's to Burger King to the jewelry kiosks. Perched in our bathrobes on the edge of the bed, my sister and I watched my father grimace at the news. He phoned his boss, Mr. Kilgore, who told him that yes, of course, my father was more than welcome to drive in and check out the store, put in some over-time; but, speaking for himself, he was planning to scramble an omelet to accompany his mimosa, smoke a Benson & Hedges, and go back to bed.

My father was concerned that Chickamauga Creek would surge across its floodplain and into the Eastgate parking lot, breach the dike of sandbags hastily thrown up by the tattooed warehouse guys the previous evening, and leak into the show-rooms. He stared out his bedroom window at the sky's furred belly, half-dressed in a V-necked T-shirt and twill trousers. A gust pummeled the sweet gums in the backyard, fierce as a riptide. A quarter mile away, the swamp had advanced to the gravel shoulder of Bonny Oaks Drive, muck splashing across the macadam, lashing eighteen-wheelers.

"A ways to go," he repeated. "Nowhere near forty days and nights."

My mother joined him at the window, her chin grazing his shoulder. She breathed in the smell of him. The lights were still on, but there were reports of outages from outlying towns like Tiftonia and Collegedale; closer in, streets in Brainerd and East Ridge were sheeted with brackish wash, their manhole covers blown off. The whole city was keyed up, edgy, apocalyptic, as when the oil tanks had exploded last year. All of us—from octogenarians languishing in a twilight at the St. Barnabas nursing home down to toddlers in Children's Church—we all knew that flood, like fire, was a sign of cataclysm, with prayer our weapon of defense. And once we prayed, trusted that the Lord would provide a solution, we were invested in the outcome, even as contradictory evidence mounted.

"Bonny Oaks will be underwater in no time. How are you going to get to Penney's?" my mother said.

"Probably Highway 58," my father said. "Higher ground that way."

"Killer, I'm scared to stay here."

He nodded his assent, clearer than spoken language. *Y'all get dressed and come along.*

In sweaters and dungarees, my sister and I sat in the Pontiac's backseat, thrilled eyewitnesses to a widening calamity. My father navigated the back streets to Highway 58, turned west to merge onto the freeway, built along a grade like the tracks of an elevated train. We could look down onto whole fields and subdivisions flooded out, roofs of duplexes like schools of whales breaching the surface. Along Brainerd Road, just shy of the mall, we drove past boarded-up bait-and-tackle shops and a darkened McDonald's, shoe outlets with muddy awnings.

At the ramp to Eastgate's parking lot, we approached a parked police sedan. An officer in thigh-high galoshes pointed to the badge on his cap. My father braked, rolled down his window, and mumbled a few words, mist beading the dashboard. The officer waved him on.

I felt something numb my back and thighs, an electric current, plugged into a celestial outlet. God wanted me to do my part. I leaned over the front seat. "Should we pray?" I said.

My mother looked back over her shoulder, her tone irritated. "Sugar, you know you should always pray."

I closed my eyes. I didn't have to say the words, I could just think them, a telepathic communiqué certain to goad Him into action. *Heavenly Father, protect us as we go into the store and please make the water go back into Chickamauga Creek and the Tennessee River.* Crisp, incisive; He'd appreciate that. *In Jesus' Name, Amen.*

My father parked the car on a dry parcel of the lot, some yards from Penney's glass doors. The sandbags made a trail like stepping-stones through a pond.

"Not so bad," he said. "More worried about the dock, frankly."

He was referring to the loading dock, where the ground dipped a few feet. As we climbed out of the Pontiac, I could see dirty water sloshing against the curb. We half-hopped from sandbag to sandbag to the doors, entered the lobby just outside the beauty shop. The floor was partially illuminated from Drapes and Linens back to Women's Clothes, but then a checkerboard of faulty bulbs cast Toys in full eclipse. The whole store had turned into a disquieting fun house, strobed lights jangled with inky shadows, playing tricks on the mind. There, over there . . . twenty-five yards away, a man paced, a drifter crazed by a passion to do us harm. I rubbed my eyes.

My father scanned the floor. "Don't like the look of this," he said. "All the lights should be on." He pointed to his left, toward Indoor Furniture, a cubicle with a cash register and a desk and a telephone. "Y'all stay here. Cholly, I'll call you on that extension." He receded between racks of polyester dresses and pleated pantsuits, leaping over ankle-deep water, arms windmilled to keep his balance. Then the darkness swallowed him, like a man falling horizontally into a cave.

My mother sat behind the desk and rummaged in her purse for a paperback Harlequin. My sister and I wandered toward

Indoor Furniture, segmented into four alcoves, each arranged like the room of a house. We pulled off our shoes and tucked the laces inside, stretched onto the living room's sofa in a pretend sleep, my damp sock against her cheek. For a moment we fake-snored. I poked her jaw with my big toe.

"Stop it," she said. "Your feet stink."

We squirmed off the sofa, looked around. There was a coffee table, an origami of beveled glass, and beyond the sofa, a china cabinet and a table shrouded in voile, a bowl of plastic violets as a centerpiece. Four chairs, ideal for a symmetrical family: father, mother, brother, sister. I could feel their love washing through this space.

The living room blended into the kitchen, drawing me deeper into a story. Here they'd eat their meals, pot roast and a lazy Susan with creamed spinach and succotash, corn on the cob. They'd laugh around the table, faces shining with piety, towheaded children reciting Bible verses to impress their doting parents.

They'd follow the script to the letter, from baptism through Bible Drill through Youth Week through Baptist college, seminary for the select few; salt of the earth, pillars of the community, envied for their stellar church attendance, their zeal for preaching the Gospel to the unsaved (extra credit points if the convert was Catholic or a double gold star if Jewish). Not like the Muldares down the street, with a dilapidated porch and a foul-smelling septic tank in the yard, a slew of lard-assed teenagers who cussed and drank Pabst and raced dirt bikes along trails behind the Red Food store; not like the Watkinses, who came to church sporadically, the boy-gaga daughter and the elfin son ostracized after Mr. Watkins left their mother for another man. No, *this* family would face each test of adversity—flood or drought, fire or blizzard—with grace and God's guidance, the empathy they'd reveal in word and deed, eyes misted with affection for each other. One episode of life would flow seamlessly into the next even as these alcoves flowed, living room to dining room to kitchen to bedroom.

I yanked open the door of a refrigerator. On the lower shelf, someone had stacked some ceramic blocks, each one painted to resemble a condiment: French's mustard, Heinz ketchup, Hellmann's mayonnaise. I shut the door. My sister had found a wet bar and three stools. She swiveled on the nearest one. "Wheeeeeee," she said, unconvincingly.

I ventured into the master bedroom. Each item was stickered with a yellow price tag. An armoire, tears of varnish clinging to its brass handles. The father's suits would hang here. A woman's vanity, with a well for face creams, a magnifying mirror; I imagined her spraying perfume from an atomizer, blowing kisses toward her outsize reflection as her son and daughter marveled on either side, mouths open. A king-size bed, larger than my parents'; I swung a leg over the edge and bounced. The mattress was firm. My sister climbed on and we shadowboxed and then she tumbled off.

My mother glanced up from her book. "You okay, Dollbaby?" she said.

We fell onto the floor in a giggling heap. We owned copies of most of these pieces, purchased with my father's discount: bucket chairs, chifforobes, floor lamps with crocheted shades. Each alcove was a diorama with only the real people missing, a chapter in a book devoid of characters, but I could fill in the blanks: parents sheltering their children, God sheltering the parents, a divinely inspired order. His Ears tuned to any plaintive cry for help, glorious concentric circles leading higher and higher . . .

The phone rang. My sister squealed. My mother picked up the receiver. "Yes, Killer," she said. "Oh, okay." She placed the receiver back in its cradle.

"What now?" my sister said.

"Y'all put your shoes on this instant," my mother said. "Your daddy's coming back."

We were standing just inside the glass doors as my father emerged from Housewares. The lights on the far side of the store were still extinguished. He was wearing a pair of gloves streaked with mud. "Good news," he said. "Sandbags held out the water pretty good. Some got in around the dock, but the men can pump it out."

"When?" my mother said.

"Over the weekend. I'll check with Mr. Kilgore." He peeled off the gloves and wrung them out in a pail one of the janitors had buttressed against the doorjamb. "Gary'll put those away," he said.

His work done, he was determined to head home. Outside he bolted the doors with a padlock and chain. The creek had drowned the parking lot, submerging the path we'd used earlier. A wind rippled miniature whitecaps.

"Have to go around," my father said.

He motioned toward a ledge, three feet high, that zagged around the building's perimeter. A brow of cloud moved overhead, the storm's backside. He helped us up one at a time. A few yards away the water lapped into a shallow, but there was another obstacle, a moraine of sandbags cresting twenty, twenty-five feet. My father worked his feet into hollows, hands flexed like a rock climber's, gingerly scaled the tiers of bags. He reached down: first for me and then my sister and then my mother.

A moment later we paused along the summit.

It would take a week for the water to recede, bulldozers dredging cul-de-sacs in Brainerd and sanitation trucks hosing stagnant water from streets downtown, near Ross's Landing. For days Chickamauga Creek would glisten, noxious, fanning its oily rainbows along golf courses, fairways transformed into straits and bays, tees and greens, archipelagoes picketed with fluttering flags.

Years from now, during a vacation from college, I'd stand in this exact spot on a cloudless noon, an unseasonably cool wind blowing from the west, as the moon wheeled in front of the sun's face, light thickening to a smoky molasses, with Penney's customers mulling around in the parking lot, peering up, faces warped and bruised like Picasso portraits. I'd understand the eclipse as portentous, something apart from me, with a prayer the only tool to ward off the threats that besieged a sterling family.

We're all praying every night before we go to bed. As your daddy says, prayer is the absolute best way we can support you.

Our Father, who art in Heaven, hallowed be Thy Name.

In the moment before we descended, the wind cracked its bullwhip, strangling the words I murmured in my head.

3

DEATH OF
A DENTIST

My mother decided she was going to fix my overbite. Last year's project had been my nearsightedness, and once convinced of the problem—that I wasn't faking poor vision just because I wanted glasses like my father's bifocals—she'd hauled me to the ophthalmologist's office, where I slumped in a vinyl chair and struggled to read ever-diminishing columns of vowels and consonants and numerals. A few weeks later we'd picked up my wire-framed glasses. "Self-improvement can be a wonderful thing, Sugar," she'd said. "Next year we're going to do something about those buck teeth." She'd made a face, lips pulled back in a chipmunk grin.

Dr. Elliott agreed with her. At my annual teeth cleaning last fall, he'd mentioned that my mother ought to consider braces for me, or at the very least a retainer. After school let out at the end of May, she drove me across Chickamauga Dam to his office on Chattanooga's north side. On the way she lectured me on how lucrative a dentistry career could be: Dr. Elliott lived with his family in a rambling house, out near Gold Point

Marina, where we kept our boat. She spoke of him admiringly, as she always did professional people. As Seventh-Day Adventists, the Elliotts attended services on Saturdays and Wednesdays rather than Sundays and Wednesdays, like the Baptists, but they basically believed everything we believed.

"Not like those Mormons," she said. "That's a false religion."

The receptionist escorted me back into Dr. Elliott's examination room, where I sat upright on his reclined chair, nervously eyeing his tray of dental tools and the enamel spit sink. He walked in, dark hair slick with pomade, a paunch beneath his scrubs. He was carrying a metal jaw mold rimmed with wet putty. "Good to see you, good to see you," he said. "How old are you now, eight, nine?"

"Nine," I said. "Ten in November."

"Whatcha got going on for the summer? Swimming lessons?" He squatted on a stool, scooting on its rollers as he adjusted the overhead lamp. "You'll like the retainer, trust me. Before you know it, it'll feel real natural, like a part of you. Open wide!"

I could smell coffee on his breath. He pressed the mold to the roof of my mouth, hard, kick-starting my gag reflex, then rolled back to his desk and looked over some papers on a clipboard. For five minutes I winced and teared while the putty hardened around my overbite. Dr. Elliott would use this to cast a plaster mold for the retainer, so precise that it would show the grooves in my gums.

A week later the retainer was ready, a pink plastic shell with wires that fit snugly around my back molars. "Wait till you have a picture-perfect smile," my mother said, as we lingered in Dr. Elliott's narrow lobby. I clutched the plaster mold, a souvenir. "Someday you'll thank me that you were able to avoid braces," she said as she wrote a personal check, her signature a baroque flourish of loops. She asked the receptionist to schedule an annual teeth cleaning for both my younger sister and me, some morning in July or August. She wanted it done before the start of school.

The retainer felt awkward in my mouth, especially during the church's Fourth of July barbecue at Reachout Ranch, when scraps of hamburger caught in the hinges. Tad Swope and Craig Allison had mocked the strings of saliva that collected in my mouth, provoking me to lisp like a cartoon character, *Thutt up, Tath and Craith, you thut up now!* When I complained to my mother, she shook her head. "You're imagining too much these days," she said. "Eccentric as the day is long, just like Aunt Georgia. Ignore those boys and their trash talk, hear?"

Besides, I could use the retainer to practice my diving at the Cumberland pool. My sister and I would stand on the edge near the deep end and I'd spit it out and hand it to her. She'd pinch it, grimacing, until I'd give her the word: she'd toss it as I hurled forward, chin tucked, thumbs locked above my head. Chlorine tickling my nose, I'd stroke down to intercept the retainer as it drifted toward the bottom, elegant as a brooch. I'd swim to the side and click it back into place, ignoring my sister's histrionics—*Eeuuw, gross, you don't know how many kids have peed in this pool*—and feeling whole again but not sure why that should be the case.

At first my mother seemed annoyed when she got the call from the dentist's office, the receptionist canceling our teeth cleaning because of a vague emergency. "Some kid hit in the mouth with a softball, I guarantee," she said. But then her mood lightened. My father had the day off; my sister and I had earned our Minnow badges the previous week; the sky was warm and cloudless.

She made a picnic lunch—a pimento cheese sandwich for my sister, deviled ham for me, leftover drumsticks for the two adults, a jumbo bag of Lay's potato chips—and tucked each cellophaned item into the cooler along with some paper napkins. She filled a thermos with Pepsi and ice cubes and a lemon wedge. After ordering us into our swimsuits, she changed into her bikini top, donning one of my father's faded dress shirts to wear to the marina. When she emerged from her bathroom, with her bleached hair and high cheekbones, she was a dead ringer, as she liked to tell people, for Barbara Stanwyck in *Double Indemnity.*

She twirled a beach towel into a snake, snapped it against my leg. "You get the day off, too," she said. "No retainer. You can soak it in that fluoride Dr. Elliott gave us."

We drove toward the lake with the windows rolled down, radio blaring that Donna Fargo song, "The Happiest Girl in the Whole USA," until the news came on and my mother clicked off the dial, claiming she was sick and tired of hearing about Watergate. From the rear seat, my sister sang the recent Dolly Parton hit:

Jolene, Jolene, Jolene, Jolene,
I'm begging of you, please don't take my man.

Across the dam we veered right onto Gann Store Road—here the houses thinned out between far-flung subdivisions and the gated Lakeshore Apartments, an outpost of luxury. The inlets glittered through breaks in the scrim of pines.

We parked in the clay lot, strolled past the cabin that housed the marina's office and down a fitful path skirted with ragweed to a weathered clapboard dock. The Cobia bobbed in its slot, nineteen feet long and technically seaworthy. We climbed aboard. After a quick inspection, my father pitched away the mooring and the boat eased into the cove. The motor chugged to life, 120 ponies' worth of power, an odor of gasoline and a blue fume. He maneuvered around the buoys and out into Lake Chickamauga's main channel. The traffic picked up like cars on I-75: catamarans, sailboats, houseboats, dinghies, a roil of competing wakes.

We merged with the flow and then left it a few miles up the lake, venturing into a backwater of Harrison Bay. Twenty yards from shore, my father killed the engine, dropped anchor. My mother told us we should swim now. She insisted on life jackets. I stepped down the ladder and backstroked into deeper water. My sister appeared on the bow, swaddled in orange cushions, toes curled, a drawn-out moment of hesitation . . . and then she was splashing near me. I stroked over and dunked her, held her down a beat and released her. She yelped and snorted into my face.

"Gro-o-o-o-s," I said.

"You deserve that," my mother admonished me. "Let me know if he tries that again, Dollbaby, and he's grounded till Labor Day."

For the next hour, my sister and I swam around the stern and then waded ashore, where we pulled crowns off goldenrods. We fell into a quarrel about a catfish carcass we found among discarded diesel cans. My mother watched from the boat, pretending not to watch. Eventually we splashed back to the Cobia and mounted the ladder. A sunburn bloomed along my neck.

After we ate, my father collected the trash in a plastic bag and knotted it over the Cobia's dashboard. He wore a placid look beneath his visor. He fired up the outboard motor and steered us back into the main channel. Just outside Gold Point's cove, we felt a shudder as the Cobia yawed. The motor died in a whirl of smoke.

"I swanny," my mother said.

We all leaned over the back of the boat. An orange slick blotted the water, muck churned up from the bottom. We'd strayed just a few feet from the dredged channel, but it was enough to cause disaster: my father pulled up the motor to reveal clots of sludge around the propeller, a chipped blade.

"Son of a gun," he said. "Should have stuck close to the buoys. Sometimes you forget this is a man-made lake. Son of a *gun*."

We were floating about fifty yards from shore, opposite Gold Point's cragged peninsula. Water moccasins had bored holes into the muddy bank, empty sockets watching, watching. My father retrieved an oar from the storage bin, bent over the side to lower it, perpendicular, testing the depth.

"Doesn't touch," he said. "But I bet the bottom's close here, maybe five feet."

During the Great Depression, the Tennessee Valley Authority had dammed the river upstream from Chattanooga, creating Lake Chickamauga, one of its larger reservoirs. President Roosevelt had spoken at the dam's dedication. As the lake filled in, it erased a string of rural communities, soybean and tobacco farms; and while the displaced farmers had been compensated for their lost land and moved to higher ground, rumors persisted that some diehards had remained. The skeletons of old barns and country churches were believed to loom just beneath the surface in Harrison Bay and Wolftever Creek.

Through the tannic water I could almost see the clapboard houses below us, filmed with moss and bellied out like aquariums, floors rotting beneath a caul of mud and the dormers silted. A steeple piercing the murky water, marking the outline of a church and a drowned cemetery. Perhaps the dead lived there still, trapped in a crypt of half lake and half land, staring up as the Cobia skimmed over them.

But I was imagining so much these days.

For two hours we paddled toward Gold Point. By four o'clock we'd reached the marina and battened down the boat and toweled off. My father trudged up to the office to report the damage to the propeller. By four-thirty we were heading south across Chickamauga Dam. Whistling a Glenn Miller tune, "String of Pearls," my father flipped on the radio. The usual big band program had been preempted by breaking news.

Recapping the latest developments: Robert P. Elliott, a prominent dentist and orthodontist from Hixson, was abducted from his home late last night by masked men and taken away in his car. His wife and three sons were left behind, unharmed. County police believe they've recovered the car in a wooded area near Sale Creek.

We listened all the way home. The reports hadn't yielded much information, just the abandoned Buick on a country road, but even my sister and I understood that the situation was serious. A dread was building as my father parked the station wagon and we unloaded the boat gear and the cooler. My parents' faces had set into identical scowls.

In the kitchen, my father turned on the clock radio: there was speculation about a ransom notice, how it would be delivered. I retreated down the hall into my bedroom, where I collapsed onto the lower bunk and hugged my stuffed tiger and whispered my fears to it, also my hopes.

"Bet the ransom phone call happens real soon," I said aloud. "They pay the money and Dr. Elliott gets to come home. Simple as that."

A rap on my door. I glanced up to see my mother, still wearing my father's faded shirt, cheeks dewed with tears.

Over the next two years, she'd quietly absorb the particulars, jot down notes on a legal pad she kept in her mahogany desk. Like a court stenographer, she'd compile the story as it grew in shocking, ridiculous proportion, poring over newspaper accounts, setting up TV trays in the den so she could tune in to the six o'clock news. With each plot twist she'd reconsider the through line in light of the books she knew—Harlequin romances; the James Michener paperbacks she shelved in her closet; and the Bible, of course—but all this thinking would only gouge out a hollow in her, bleeding off something she'd always believe to be immutable. She'd wonder how Dr. Elliott's death could fit into a moral universe so plainly mapped out in each worship service, in each stirring sermon and lusty hymn. She'd stumbled across some untidy, buried truth, something she felt compelled to excavate, shattered into bits that she'd painstakingly join together again, like a jigsaw puzzle, to reveal the image.

Now, though, she responded in the only way that made sense to her. "Down on your knees, Sugar, we need to pray for Dr. Elliott's family," she said. "How could anyone do something like this to such a nice lady?" She wiped her eyes with the heel of her hand.

⌒⌒◯

My ears felt plugged. Her voice rippled toward me, gargly and underwater, dings of sonar in an oceanic trench. *Down on your knees, Sugar, we need to pray.*

Prayer: it floated you across the lake in your mind, pillowed by gentle currents and the dreams of the dead.

But I was imagining too much these days.

⌒⌒◯

At the trial, the dentist's wife took the witness stand, surrendering to the district attorney's barrage of probing questions. He'd coughed and harrumphed as she pieced together the sequence of events. There'd been a tense pause before he launched into his line of inquiry. She'd sat there, impervious to his implications, her hands balled in her lap as she strained to recall some elusive detail or gesture that would shift the narrative, bring the confused jumble into bright, clarifying focus.

What she remembered was this:

They'd left the midweek prayer meeting in a solemn mood, as the sermon had used Revelation as its text. All that talk of Judgment Day had sparked a migraine behind her eyes. In the Buick's backseat, the boys had sat like toy soldiers, ramrod-stiff, the two older ones holding their library books, with the four-year-old sandwiched between them, his eyes drowsy slits. When they first pulled out of the Seventh-Day Adventists' parking lot, her husband had made small talk about the day's business, the root canals and molar cavities, but then he'd lapsed into a brooding silence. He'd rolled down the Buick's windows to funnel in air, humid and fragrant with honeysuckle. This had surprised her. He usually flipped on the air conditioner, as his tastes were anything but frugal.

They'd stopped by the Red Food store for groceries and then headed across the dam, where the city's outskirts had washed up a flotsam of subdivisions. Later she tried to recall whether she'd felt any foreboding, a tightening in the gut, but she could only summon an image like a photograph, flat and unrevealing: the slope of Fairview Road, the house's silhouette, each window darkened, a few stars snared in the fringes of the loblolly pines along the drive. The stench of the lake a mile away, beyond Gold Point Marina.

Nothing suspicious, except that the garage light was out.

He noticed this. He parked the Buick and got out to inspect it. She swung open the passenger door, balancing a sack of tomatoes against her hip. Something in his manner caused her to halt on the sidewalk. The boys had tumbled from the backseat, irritable, and were huddled around the front door when he joined her.

"Light's busted out. Not sure how that happened."

He turned the key in the lock and stepped aside as she hesitated. Behind her, her older sons had started a game of Rock, Paper, Scissors to see who would walk the garbage down the driveway. In the kitchen, just off the foyer, she set the tomatoes down on a counter. A noise startled her: from the adjacent dining room, a man approached, a knit ski mask tight over his face, aiming a shotgun toward her. The four-year-old screamed and lunged at her skirt, but she instinctively pushed him away, as she'd do to a dog with muddy paws. The child darted past his brothers, knocking open the half-closed door, and into the night.

Another man, also wearing a ski mask and gripping a pistol, bolted from a pool of shadow near the bottom of the stairs and through the door. She heard him curse down the drive: "Get back here, you little shit." She guessed the child heeded the command, because she heard the man's voice again, nearer, just outside the door. "Your parents done taught you how to obey, you little shit. Can't say the same for my old man and lady."

She dallied in the doorway between the foyer and the kitchen, poised on a bridge between her former life and the next. The first man banged the door shut with his fist and nodded to her, an act of familiarity that felt presumptuous, invasive. She was amazed at their racket, given that her neighbors would all be home from church. The other man herded her husband and three sons down the hall. She still hadn't seen her husband's face since he'd looked so perplexed on the driveway, peering up at the damaged light. The first man—the tall, burly one—waved the shotgun's barrel in the direction of the living room. She walked slowly, arms at her sides.

The two older boys stood in front of the couch, quite pale. Her husband held his hands above his head, something he'd seen on *Adam-12* and *Hawaii Five-0*. His fingers jittered, the opposite of the usual control he showed when handling a drill or a screwdriver. She sat primly on the La-Z-Boy recliner and pulled the four-year-old into her lap, her hand tangled in the child's hair while he cowered.

"There's some jewelry upstairs," her husband said. "Back of my wife's closet. A mink coat, you can take that as well."

"Get the fuck down on the ground," the tall man said.

Her husband knelt on the braided rug, his suit jacket slipping from his shoulder. The tall man kicked him, and he fell forward, striking the coffee table and upending a crystal candy dish. The smaller man trained the pistol at her husband's head while his partner disappeared upstairs.

"A mink coat," her husband said again, facedown on the floor. "A gun in a hatbox, back of the closet. There may be some cash in the bottom drawer of the armoire."

"You said a gun?" the man asked. She could see that the lip of his mask was damp with saliva. "Don't you dare move." He withdrew down the hall and from the foot of the stairs yelled up to his partner.

A moment later both men came into the living room. The tall man had draped her coat over his arm and beneath it an ermine stole, the one she wore to church on Christmas and Easter. He was carrying her husband's duffel bag, zipped up—she assumed he'd stuffed it with her pearls and gold chokers and costume jewelry. His partner held a beige pillowcase with yarn tassels.

"We're taking a hostage," he said.

"I'll go, take me," her husband said, his voice muffled from the shag carpet.

One of the men asked her husband to stand. She glanced up to see his face, chalky with fright, as the pillowcase swallowed it. The older boys were sobbing now as the tall man shoved her husband down the entry hall. From her vantage point she could see him buckle and stagger back to his feet. The shorter man slouched against the china cabinet, twirling the pistol John Wayne–style, raised the tip to his forehead to salute her.

"Wait a good long while before you call the police," he said. "Wait for, oh, an hour and fifteen minutes."

He saluted her again. She stood and guided her youngest son to the couch, where she wedged herself among all three boys while they cried, burrowing into her, their faces wetting her blouse. She could see the front door still ajar, and heard the slam of the Buick's trunk. She knew her husband was claustrophobic.

She lifted her chin to meet the ski mask with a resigned, dry-eyed stare. "I understand," she said.

"An hour and fifteen minutes," he said again and backed down the hall and closed the door gently.

At the trial, the prosecutor and detectives puzzled over the curious timeframe, what it could have meant in the larger scheme of the murder. They calculated that the trip up the highway—past Lake Chickamauga's coves and man-made archipelago, to Montlake Road, where they'd recovered the Buick and its grisly treasure the following afternoon—would have lasted maybe half an hour. When interrogated, she didn't have an explanation, even when more details emerged, and her own role was called into question.

After the killers were sentenced, she revisited the night's events with a sour diligence. For that hour and fifteen minutes she had seemed to rise slightly as she'd repeatedly checked the grandfather clock. A day of reckoning had come, as she'd been promised in church. When the time limit had expired, she'd remained on the couch, relaxing her embrace, calmly aware that there was no need to rush for help, no emergency number to dial. The phone lines had been cut.

Two summers later—the Bicentennial summer—my new dentist announced that I no longer needed the retainer.

"That's great news, Sugar!" my mother said when I greeted her in Dr. Ratchford's lobby, the retainer sealed off in a plastic bag like a relic from an archaeological dig. "No need for braces, ever!" At the lobby door, she twined her hand in the red, white, and blue bunting the receptionist had taped there. She looked at me sternly, paraphrased the verse from the Gospel of Luke: "From those to whom much is given, much is expected."

My mother had mentioned Dr. Elliott only occasionally: first, when there had been a break in the criminal investigation and two contract killers had been arrested; and then during the sensational trial, which had captured headlines for weeks. Among the revelations: an insurance policy worth nearly a million dollars, a blood feud between another dentist and Dr. Elliott, sworn testimony that implicated his wife and mother-in-law. Although investigators were never able to connect Mrs. Elliott directly to the crime, my mother remained convinced she'd orchestrated it, a woman seething with some mysterious conflict, a blind, mute revolt against the conventions of her life.

"How could such a nice lady do this?" she'd say, shaking her head as if she'd reached some inevitable conclusion. "Well, the Adventists were never that close to God anyway."

She never brought up Dr. Elliott again. The Bicentennial came and went, a flurry of barbecues and fireworks, a gala church service with a patriotic sermon and the handbell choir clanging out the anthem "Let Christ's Freedom Ring!" My mother coaxed my father to sell the Cobia, then sell our house and buy a larger one across town, a Spanish-style adobe with decorative iron grates around each window, a yucca planted next to the mailbox, and miles away from the lake, with its smells of fish and diesel oil, its mosquitoes and its secrets. "Mi casa es su casa!" she joked as she wrapped plates in old newspaper, striking a pose, holding a couple of saucers like castanets.

Amid the welter of packed crates and rolled carpets and moving vans, she stayed focused on her family's self-improvement, right down to the vexing imperfections of her buck-toothed, nearsighted son. This summer's project involved contact lenses. The ophthalmologist had fitted me for a pair of tiny hard lenses on account of my age and the fact that they required less daily care than soft. "They'll feel natural in no time, like your eyeballs," my mother assured me the afternoon we picked up the lenses, snug in the cups of their case. "I hated the way those durned glasses slipped to the end of your nose."

Safely ensconced in the new house, I spread out a towel next to the sink in the hall bathroom, along with a plastic bottle of saline and a compact, practiced inserting the lenses directly onto the pupils. If I dropped one, I could find it on the cloth, a fleck of blue against a swath of white. I suffered the sting of excessive tearing, but gradually the irritation eased, opening up my field of vision as I rode a bike down side streets and around cul-de-sacs, glancing over my shoulder at neighbors as they receded.

Sometimes I'd forget I'd put the lenses in. At the Cumberland pool, I'd dive into the deep end and crab along the bottom, peering up through goggles at the surface's concave mirror, the beluga thighs of older women, wreaths of bubbles kicked up by the Minnow swim class. A world sharper and crisper than I'd ever imagined.

4

THE TAMEKA PROBLEM

Miss Eula Givens, the church organist, snapped her wrists across the keys, quivering the final arpeggio of "All to Jesus I Surrender." She glanced up from the sheet music and smiled that thin-lipped, chilly smile so particular to her she could have patented it. The choir remained standing in the loft behind her. A light rinsed through the sanctuary's stained-glass windows, blue and gauzy, as the congregation cleared its collective throat impatiently, eager to disperse to the noon meal, Shoney's Big Boy or Morrison's or the Tick Tock Restaurant, over on Ringgold Road.

Brother Roy opened his robed arms like the image of Christ the Redeemer I'd seen in the encyclopedia, the statue that sanctified the harbor in Rio de Janeiro. "Brothers and sisters," he said, his tone shifting from sermon to announcement mode. "I'm delighted to present Miss Tameka Wilson, who's come this morning to profess her faith in the redemptive grace of our Lord." Tameka—fifteen, surly, chin ducked—fell awkwardly into his embrace. Instantly scores of thought balloons shot up, tethered in a communal synapse.

Why, she's a black girl.

Never been done.

A speck of pepper in a sea of salt.

There's room for her at the AME or the Temple of Lift Jesus Up—why would she want to join here?

Tameka cowered against Brother Roy's sleeve, hair teased into a clipped Afro, muscled arms bursting beneath the spaghetti straps of her sundress. She scowled, eyes lowered toward the carpet, feeling the hurricane blast of disapproval, invisible but potent, Category 5. As a ward of the Children's Home, out on Lee Highway, she was entitled to worship at the church of her choice; and because Mr. Buford, the home's director, was a member of our congregation, she'd asked to join as well. She'd been coming to services and youth activities for nearly a year. Except for her skin pigmentation, she fit the profile of the other teenagers who poured out of Mr. Buford's van when he'd pull up to the colonnade: gawky, dressed in acrylic hand-me-downs from Goodwill, and clutching donated Living Bibles, bindings cracked, gilt lettering flaked, illegible.

"Tameka has asked Jesus into her heart, stands before us today as a little sister in Christ," Brother Roy said. "Can't think of a reason not to proceed to the ordinance of baptism."

After the service we stopped by McDonald's on Brainerd Road. My mother commandeered one of the tables outside, next to the playground, its umbrella an inverted tulip shielding us against the May heat. She drummed her fingers on the concrete surface, grilling my sister about who said what in Sunday School, and had she remembered to turn in her tithe? Through the plate-glass windows, I watched my father as he paced at the counter, mouth tight, waving his hands in front of the black teenager who'd taken his order. I'd asked for a cheeseburger without onions, a special request that had caused a delay.

A moment later he emerged, red-faced, ferrying a couple of grease-splotched paper bags. "Why can't they understand plain English?" he said. Shaking her head, my mother doled out the contents, Big Macs and milk shakes and pouches of French fries, the offending cheeseburger. My sister jabbed a straw through the lid of her Coke.

"Every time they get the order wrong," my father said. "Have to start over. Really ticks me off."

My mother tucked a McNugget in the purse of her mouth, eyes slanted with self-righteous consternation. She chewed methodically. "This Tameka problem," she said. "Not sure what to do."

"We have to vote on her," my father said.

I knew what he meant. There were three paths to church membership: Letters of Recommendation for newly transferred families; the doctrinally abstract and rarely used Statement of Faith; Profession of Faith for the newly saved, often children or adolescents.

At the close of each service, Brother Roy would announce the invitational hymn, hoping to rake in new recruits. In the first scenario, a family, just moved from Knoxville or Spartanburg, would present letters from their previous pastor, attesting to impeccable moral credentials. The Statement of Faith was a catchall, usually tailored for an older woman—often a fresh divorcée in her forties or fifties, humiliated when her husband ditched her for a younger, slimmer version, who couldn't bear the thought of worshiping at her Presbyterian or Methodist church even one more Sunday, scalded by the pitying looks of women and men she'd known her whole life—to bypass baptism and the rigorous (some said brainwashing) New Members' class by simply stating she believed the things the Baptists believed, and always had.

In a typical Profession of Faith, a boy would stand timidly before the congregation and admit in a quavering voice that he'd asked Jesus into his heart and that he'd like to become a member—I'd done this at the age of seven, and my sister a couple of years later, along with the Sanders girls and Tad Swope and Mandy Welch.

This child comes before you to publicly declare her belief in the grace shown by Our Lord on the Cross . . . Circle your loving arms around her as a sister in Christ.

Simple as pie.

Each candidate would be ratified in the monthly business meeting, held during the sparsely attended Wednesday night service: a show of hands, an acclamation of *aye*. A formality, nothing more.

"We have to vote on her," my father said. Which I interpreted as voting Tameka down, something that had never happened before.

My mother dabbed a froth of chocolate from her lips. "Sounds fair to me," she said, her resistance to Tameka hardening, like a seam of igneous rock.

But they hadn't counted on Brother Roy. From his pulpit, he trained his psychic radar across the pews below him, sussing out the weak-willed, locking in on the recalcitrant: older deacons, grumbling about an overreach of executive authority; the dowagers, Miss Eula and Miss Netta Barnstable, the director of the Women's Missionary Union, esteemed for their cruel propriety; the core families, like ours, who could vote in whomever they liked. These he lobbied with his sunny charm and appeals to good sense, pigeonholing them in the men's room, the Fellowship Hall. "Tameka has had a difficult life," he'd say. "Abandoned. She's blossomed under the nurturing hands of the Bufords." He'd lasso an arm around a firm shoulder, crack a grin that telegraphed his authority. "For all of her problems, I see the spirit of Christ in her," he'd say, multiple meanings churning beneath the sentiment.

As in *Red and yellow, black and white: they are precious in His sight.*

As in *No bigots allowed in my flock, you hear?*

As in *What you know—and what I know you know—is that the color of Christ's skin was likely closer to hers than to yours, paleface.*

Something else was left unsaid, something we never broached: our denomination owed its existence to the subjugation of black people. In the years preceding the Civil War, Baptists in the South had diverged from their Northern brethren, insisting that slave-owning planters deserved prominent positions in the church hierarchy, a notion anathema to the abolitionists of New England. The Southern clergy increasingly invoked the Bible to justify slavery, convening a conference in Augusta, Georgia, in 1845, when they severed their ties and declared themselves the Southern Baptist Convention, an institution that had thrived throughout Reconstruction and the Jim Crow era. Subsequent generations of African-Americans hadn't exactly felt comfortable among the Baptists, those pews jammed with hoards of towheaded, blue-eyed worshipers. As recently as the late 1960s, only a minuscule percentage of individual churches even permitted African-Americans to join.

The congregation bowed to Brother Roy's wishes, voting Tameka in. I wondered if she had intuited the antagonism, deep as an ocean trench. He'd dunked her at the tail end of one group baptism so as to downplay the event. In the baptistery, she'd grimaced, sinewy arms folded across her chest; after her immersion she'd climbed the stairs, shoulders arched, water beaded and glistening in her hair.

In the end, though, the congregation won the larger, silent debate. An athlete, Tameka joined the girls' basketball and softball teams. She was physically adept at knocking in her share of runs per game, or whooshing the net from midcourt, but she proved too aggressive, slinging *bitch* and *honky* at her opponents in the interdenominational league, prompting protests from the Methodists and Church of Christs.

She even exhibited hostility toward her teammates, cursing if she felt they were eclipsing her on the court. During one practice in the church gym, she'd scuffled with Trudie Parham, elbowing Trudie's jaw and blackening her eye. The next week Tameka failed to show up to her game. She skipped practices the following week as well. Her record of absenteeism spilled into Sunday School and worship services. At one Wednesday evening supper, I bumped into Mr. Buford in the serving line and asked about her, but he shook his head, indicating there was a story there but he'd keep it to himself, glory be to God.

Soon it became evident that Tameka wasn't coming back. Months stretched into a year, then two. Her face remained, blurred but with a discernible frown, in that year's girls' basketball team photo on display in the trophy case outside Brother Roy's office. Mrs. Tomlinson, the church secretary, eventually dropped her from the rolls, typing over her name with a series of Xs. Soon we forgot about her, a soul rubbed out but leaving a trace of herself behind, frowning, a palimpsest.

"Wanna hear something cool?" Craig Allison said, leaning so close his chin brushed my shoulder, his voice low but squeaky, like Mickey Mouse's. "I have sperm." His lips curled into a sanctimonious *s*.

"What?"

"I've got sperm."

We were standing beneath the canopy that shaded the entrance to the church basement. Our fourth-grade teacher, Mrs. Massie, had been saddled with late duty this week. She'd corralled a dozen younger kids just inside the glass doors and was holding forth on the virtues of an orderly line, no cusswords, no balls tossed. She hadn't noticed that Craig had lured me outside, behind the hortensia shrubs, their cobalt blue blooms plumped out like snowballs. I perched on the curb of the church's driveway, a crescent of pavement that spurred off Mayfair Avenue. A Gran Torino pulled up, the passenger door cracked open, stereo blaring Elvis Presley, *We can't go on together with suspicious minds.* A blond girl, one of the first graders, climbed in.

Two years ago our church had debuted its own academy, kindergarten through sixth grade, advertising a "Christ-centered education" in the local papers. Enrollment had grown to over a hundred students. I'd heard rumblings about court-ordered busing, racial flare-ups in the halls of public schools, but my father had assured me that I was going to church school for one primary reason: so that I could study God's Word like any other textbook, Math or English or Social Studies.

I wasn't sure what sperm was, exactly—something to do with my scrotum, pink, hairless slug that swelled in summer, when the chiggers bit down there. But I knew Craig knew. Although he and I were the same height, he commanded a larger space, bursting with bantam swagger, chest thrust out in an alpha stance. The boys in our class surfed the riptides of his moods ruefully, never daring to break free from his potty mouth and ironfisted rule. He held a trump card: he channeled an encyclopedia of worldly knowledge from his older brother, Kyle, a seventh grader at the public school on the other side of Brainerd Road. What little I'd learned about female anatomy I'd learned from Craig.

"Not sure what that is," I said.

Craig snorted, rolled his eyes theatrically. "Dork, that gooey stuff inside your dick," he said. "Makes babies." He shifted his weight from foot to foot, peered around the hortensia to see if Mrs. Massie had discovered her mistake.

"Well, you probably don't got it," he said. "Dorkiest of all dorks."

"What don't I got?"

"Clear pee." We heard a honk down Mayfair Avenue, a burgundy Monte Carlo that coasted into the driveway. Mrs. Allison was picking us up for an after-school round of pins at the Holiday Bowl on Brainerd Road. We saw her behind the wheel, opaque sunglasses like Jackie O's, the dusky complexion she'd bequeathed to both of her sons. "Hurry up," I said.

"I pee clear, that's all," he said. The Monte Carlo braked parallel to us. Mrs. Massie stormed out from under the canopy, waved for Mrs. Allison to roll down her window.

"Shirl-Jo, those boys just snuck out while I was attending to the other children," she said. She glared at me, indicating whom she considered the instigator. "In there," Craig ordered, yanking open the rear door on the passenger side. I scrambled across the vinyl white seat, Mrs. Allison smiling vaguely at me. He shut the door behind us, twisted his mouth at Mrs. Massie through the window, a clown's grimace. She clucked like a chicken as Mrs. Allison drove off, toward Brainerd Road.

He whispered in my ear. "Twice this week, in the bathroom. I unzipped and aimed at the middle of the toilet and the pee was clear as rainwater. Now I can make babies, should I choose to get a girl pregnant."

"Craig," Mrs. Allison called over her shoulder, "I got to pick up Kyle, then I'll drop you boys off."

A moment later she parked in a queue of vehicles outside the junior high school, its weathered brick walls crowned with a raggedy cupola, paint dangling in ribbons. All around us were waiting mothers, idling car pools, a mass of orange-yellow buses. "Can't say I ever seen it this busy," Mrs. Allison said. "Maybe 'cause it's so close to the end of term." She switched off the ignition, cranked down her window to admit a pillow of stale air, a skunky odor, as though some animal were dying in silent convulsions in the weedy ditches beyond the gymnasium.

Ahead of us, near the crosswalk, a flash of movement. We heard screams.

"What on earth?" Mrs. Allison said, half-standing on the floorboard and tipping three-quarters out the window.

More screams.

She kicked open the door and got out, plucked off her sunglasses for a better look. A pop like a firecracker, a puff of smoke. A boy about Kyle's age sprinted past the Monte Carlo, bumped against the side mirror but veered back into balance like quicksilver, disappeared among the cars arrayed behind us.

Mrs. Allison turned around, teeth clenched, accentuating her square jaw and beaked nose. "Listen up," she said. "You boys stay in the car, roll up the window and lock the doors."

"Too hot," Craig said. "I'll die of eggs fixation."

"Do as you're told," she snapped, "or your daddy will tan your hide when he gets home."

She walked forward, wobbly on stilettos, her hand touching the hoods and trunks for reassurance. We lost sight of her as she passed a line of anxious women, fidgeting with their rings and bandannas. A bottle rocket whirled overhead to crash in a mist of blue sparks.

"Getting good," Craig said.

"Better roll up that window and lock the doors," I said. "Do as you're told."

"Dammit to hell, would somebody please explain why I hang out with your wussy ass?" Craig said, knocking his fist against his forehead in I-coulda-had-a-V8 fashion. "Plus, your bowling sucks."

We lounged uncomfortably across the backseat. I skimmed a Fantastic Four comic book, ignoring Craig. "Clear pee," he opined out loud, "never lies." More teenagers jogged past the car, a girl in a halter dress with a daisy pattern, spattered with blood. "Ho-lee shit," he said. Then Mrs. Allison was standing there, rapping on the windshield, Kyle clinging to her waist. Craig flipped the lock on the driver's side, pushed the door ajar. His brother scooted into the passenger seat, neck damp with sweat, filling the car with his gamey scent. "Pee-yew," Craig said, pinching his nose.

"Shut up, booger monster," Kyle said, staring ahead. "Or I'll toss you to them wolves."

"Haven't seen anything like that in a while," Mrs. Allison

said, her voice flat and stunned, as though she'd just grazed an electric fence. She sat down, trembling, behind the wheel but kept the door open. "A race riot," she said. "Black girls beating up on a white girl, and then them boys got in on the act."

"Did the white girls beat up on the black girls?" I said.

She seemed not to have heard my question. "I had to do something," she murmured. "Couldn't let that poor child suffer at the hands of hooligans." She wagged a finger at me. "Cholly woulda done the same thing."

From somewhere behind us a gunshot, or an engine's backfire. Screams.

"This is why y'all go to Christian school," she said, hands covering her eyes. "So you won't have to deal with this."

The fracas surged closer. Through the open door, I saw more teenagers rushing past us, hurling knapsacks and books to the curb, slugging each other, a flurry of fists and chins. More smoke bombs detonated on the school lawn, scrolling a dirty fog. A white boy flailed like a marionette on the pavement next to the car, his limbs lolling at odd angles, a blur of tie-dyed T-shirt and cutoff Levi's. A black girl in a turquoise dashiki dove into the hood, clutching her side, fingers curved around the ornament. She winced, breathing hard, but cheeks clean of tears: the face of Tameka in the photo outside of Brother Roy's office.

At that moment I knew the Tameka Problem would always be with us. We could go anywhere and it would sniff us out, in church services and dive bars, in corporate boardrooms and film studios, on wheat farms and basketball courts. Mrs. Allison sobbed but still didn't close the door. "What the hell? What the hell?" Kyle muttered, over and over, but no one could answer his question. The light changed again, yellow as a lesion;

sirens wailed their Doppler panic. Craig and I held hands, the Monte Carlo a bulwark against the bodies swirling around us. Somewhere beyond our city, a cyclone seethed across a continent, angrier than any storm we'd seen, mauling the innocent and the guilty: gritty ghettos, down-on-their-luck towns, the groomed fairways of country clubs. Abandoned pueblos out west, where no one saw it coming, where no one mounted the cliff ladders in fear, where scarves of hummingbirds still blessed the air.

5

PERSEPHONE IN NEW MEXICO

To test my self-restraint, I'd been saving *D'Aulaires' Book of Greek Myths* for when July bleared into August, long after the tennis lessons were done and just before our church group loaded into a Greyhound for a pilgrimage to Glorieta, the Baptist conference center outside of Santa Fe, New Mexico, its stucco dormitories strewn across the foothills of the Sangre de Cristo Mountains. On days when the weather proved too sweltering for even a sprint through the sprinklers, I'd loll on the couch in the basement, luxuriating in the air-conditioning and drinking in the old stories, illustrations so fluorescent they could have appeared in a medieval manuscript. The Olympians fascinated me most: Poseidon with his earthquakes; Dionysus transforming mutinous sailors into dolphins; jealous Hera sending a gadfly to torment the hapless heifer Io. Volatile, tragic Demeter, forced to relinquish her daughter, Persephone, to Hades for the winter months, tilting the earth into cold, barren shadow while Persephone sat enthroned in the

Underworld, silent among the whispering ghosts and brittle sapphires and rubies.

My mother decided I shouldn't spend those muggy days before Glorieta with my nose in a book. She urged my father to come up with a father-son project. At first we practiced baseball catches in the backyard, but the heat did us in, along with the mosquitoes and no-see-ums. An indoor project: that was the thing.

Last year we'd tried collecting coins, but he'd ended up doing all the work, inserting tarnished silver dollars into cardboard sleeves, negotiating on the phone with dealers in Kansas and Wisconsin. With that failed effort fresh in mind, he aimed for something a boy might like better, something more tactile. He bought a stone-polishing kit from a vendor who supplied costume jewelry to Penney's. He set it up in the basement, near an outlet: a rotor with an extension cord, tubes of unguent chemicals, a rubber drum that could rotate for weeks on a low current of electricity. The machine whirred, a *grg-grg-grg-grg* that sounded like a stick-shift truck stuck between gears. He explained that together we'd create lustrous gems from crude stones, a process that might earn us a berth at the annual crafts fair at the mall. He dropped a few pieces of gravel into the drum to demonstrate, flicked on the switch, *grg-grg-grg-grg*.

"Killer, he's eleven years old," my mother said. She was standing in the middle of the basement, sweating in a faded red bikini, sipping a glass of iced tea. She'd spent the afternoon in her chaise lounge on the patio, slathered with tanning oil and bug spray, skimming Fern Michaels and Victoria Holt romances. "About to start sixth grade. I mean, why *rocks*?" She frowned, skeptical.

"He's a nerd," my sister said laconically from her post in

front of the television set. She flopped belly-down on the shag carpet, chin propped on her elbows, blond hair crosshatched in a French braid.

"A what?" my mother said. "Dollbaby, he's a character, I grant you that, but every family has one. Reminds me a bit of Aunt Georgia, although no one could ever hold a candle to *her*."

"A nerd," my sister said without turning her head. "Always quoting from the Bible and books, telling us what to do. *Blessed are the poor in spirit: for theirs is the kingdom of heaven.* Goes on and on. You should hear the kids at church laugh."

"Shut up," I said. "Not very Christian of you."

"All the Beatitudes, all the time. None of us want him for a team. Can't even throw a ball."

"What did I tell you about saying 'shut up,' Sugar?" my mother said.

"Now it's those dang Greek myths," my sister said, still staring at the television screen. "Hoo boy."

"Better get that out of your system before New Mexico, missy," my mother said. "What would Brother Roy say if you said 'dang' on the bus?"

"Crafts fair's in October." My father clicked the rotor off, picked up the drum, and shook it like a tambourine. "Very durable," he said.

Under his tutelage I started simple: agate. Some samples had come with the kit. I tucked the chalked stones into the drum along with a powder of silicon carbide, the grinding medium, and some water from the garden hose. The drum turned over and over for ten days. In the next stage I drained the drum's contents through a strainer, filtering the half-buffed stones from a slurry of grit. After rinsing out the drum with

Palmolive, I thrust the stones back inside with a fine tin oxide that would yield glistening, oblong gems, some flattened into bands of amber and russet, some rippled like bacon. As my father explained, once I'd mastered the technique, I could move on to the stones found at the crafts show like wares at a bazaar: amethyst, jasper, aventurine, obsidian, even chips of fossilized wood. In time—not this year, but maybe next—I could attempt the ultimate prize, the tiger's-eye, coveted for money clips and earrings.

One evening the week before we left for Glorieta, Brother Roy surprised us on his way home from church. A recent widower, he now accepted invitations to supper with his congregants, all of whom had adored his wife, Sister Beryl, and felt terrible that she'd died of a coronary in her fifties. Brother Roy said that he'd just seen George and Jeannie Sanders, my parents' closest friends, and they'd mentioned our new endeavor. "I have a proposition for you," he said, grinning, his gray hair greased back and his weak chin more apparent up close. I was used to seeing him in the pulpit, bathed in a glare of spotlights. Because of his widespread reputation as a dynamic preacher, one who adhered to an old-school fire-and-brimstone technique, our church services were televised on the local station, transmitted live and in color throughout eastern Tennessee and northern Georgia and Alabama. He was the nearest I'd ever come to a celebrity, besides Billy Graham, who had preached at Memorial Auditorium when I was eight; and Pat Boone, impossibly tan, who flew in each year for the Bethel Bible School golf tournament and fund-raiser.

Out of context, though, Brother Roy seemed pale, fatigued around the eyes. My father ushered him down to the basement, where we sat on the couch, away from the whirring rotor. Brother Roy fished a bag from his briefcase and offered it to me. I unfolded the creased paper and jiggled loose the contents onto a square of chamois cloth: a dozen gray-green flakes, dull and nicked at the edges.

"I sure hope you can help me out," he said.

He wanted me to polish his jade, a souvenir from an ancient battlefield he'd visited while on a mission tour of Turkey last year. When he purchased the jade, he'd thought he might have a necklace made for Sister Beryl, a pendant or beads strung along a silver chain, but now that she'd gone home to be with the Lord, he was thinking about a bracelet for his teenage daughter. "I'll pay you a little something toward a new bike," he said, kneading my shoulder.

"No need for that," my father said hoarsely, moved by the request. "We'd be happy to do it for free. It'll give us some experience."

Jade! I felt dizzy with the trust that Brother Roy had vested in me. As we climbed the stairs back to the foyer, he engaged in light banter with my father. "Are you sure you won't take a little compensation for your efforts?" parried by "Just put in a good word for us in your prayers tonight, that's worth a down payment on a mansion in Heaven." Brother Roy paused by the front door, where my mother held his seersucker jacket, gripped my shoulder again, a gesture pregnant with rich feeling but also tinged with an exhaustive grief.

"Won't you stay for supper?" my mother said. "I thawed out the chuck roast and some snap peas, threw them into the Crock-Pot to stew. Should be ready in, oh, ten minutes."

"Cholly, you are the sweetest person to try and fatten me

up," he said, eyes crinkled. He stole the jacket from her arm, nudged the door open with his free hand. "But I got to run home and start packing for New Mexico. I bet you're ahead of me on that one!"

For nearly a week Mr. Draper had driven the Greyhound west, worrying about its many afflictions, cheerfully beeping the horn at other church buses. We'd crossed the Mississippi River at Memphis, swirls of brown water visible through the bridge's iron grates, and rolled steadily through Arkansas and Oklahoma and into the Texas Panhandle, where stands of sweet gum and live oak gave way to prairie dense with wildflowers and then to sweeps of drylands, wire grass with bald patches of dust.

In Amarillo one afternoon, we'd stopped for lunch at a cowboy-themed restaurant, all forty of us lined along common tables, waitresses scrambling for a couple of booster chairs. We'd elicited a few stares when Brother Roy blessed the meal. I'd eaten a half-pound Steerburger, garnished with mayonnaise and greasy American cheese, a heap of fried onion rings. "There's a growing boy for you," my mother had said to Mrs. Swope.

I'd brought along a duffel bag with some board games, books to while away the time—my Bible, a Golden History of the Civil War, two Chronicles of Narnia, and the *D'Aulaires' Book of Greek Myths*. I'd progressed to myths in which mortals played larger roles: Theseus, Perseus, Oedipus and the Sphinx. Orpheus, whose agony over the death of his young wife compelled him to journey with his lyre through a network of caves to the Underworld, where his exquisite music stirred Hades and Persephone to tears.

We'd experienced a couple of delays—a transmission glitch near the New Mexico state line, Mr. Norway passing a gallstone in the bathroom of a gas station in Tucumcari—but here in the final stretch we'd gained back time, forsaking the interstate for a more direct two-lane highway to Glorieta. For months now our church had planned to send a group to the annual summer conference. The list had winnowed down by attrition—can't-miss Panama City vacations, an outbreak of summer flu, and, frankly, apathy—leaving only the core of faithful, high-attendance families.

This actually pleased Brother Roy. We were his favorite people: the Sanderses and Welches and Drapers and Norways and Cains; the divorced Mrs. Swope, whose sarcasm made us all laugh; a retired couple, the Laughlins, who had brought along Marilyn, their college-age granddaughter from Kentucky, a pear-shaped hippie girl with a frizzy perm and buckskin vests and bell-bottoms with glittery appliquéd peace signs. I'd spent most of the trip at the back of the bus, enthralled, while Marilyn strummed a guitar and belted out songs in a faltering soprano, *La-a-a-ady, when you're with me I'm sm-i-ling, give me, wo-wo-wo, your lo-ove.* The verdict on Marilyn had quietly circulated, something about a fraternity keg party, her compromised virtue. I'd overheard Mrs. Welch say to my mother that we were all supposed to help out the Laughlins and keep a watchful eye on her.

In our trek west we'd risen imperceptibly, thousands of feet. Through the bus's duct-taped windows I could see the highway coil along a landscape of brush and tumbleweeds and cactuses, quasi-lunar. I stretched out on the commodious rear seat with my head in my mother's lap, my abdomen clenched with nausea. When we arrived at the Glorieta campus just after nightfall, I staggered from the bus and threw up in the parking lot adjacent to Oklahoma Hall, the stucco lodge that housed families from all over the country.

My mother quarantined me in our two-room suite. She swabbed a washcloth across my forehead when I spiked a fever, measured out teaspoons of Pepto-Bismol as I sat listlessly on the couch, shivering beneath a Navajo blanket and staring at my books on the coffee table, too feeble to open them. She wasn't inclined to fuss over me in this way. As the older boy, I was expected to take care of myself, more or less: turn in perfect report cards, slam-dunk Bible Drill, waltz through viral season with a modicum of coughs and sneezes. A laudable model of Baptist boyhood. Still, she brought me lozenges, cans of ginger ale.

By the fourth day I'd recovered, accompanied the group to the Texas Hall cafeteria for breakfast. The cafeteria's windows looked onto a mesa bristled with piñons, an ice blue lake, and the sanctuary beyond, where the entire conference gathered each evening for services. Mrs. Swope sat next to my mother. "Some bug you picked up," she said to me with her signature certitude. "Maybe hold off on them sausage links until tomorrow."

My sister spooned the last of her Rice Krispies and pushed the bowl away. "You know he's faking it," she said. She took a sip from her glass of Tang.

"How so?" Mrs. Swope said.

"Just is," my sister said, deigning to glance at me. "Likes to show off."

Faking it? I drew myself up in my chair to remind her of the lines of authority, who followed whom in the pecking order. In a haughty tone I delivered a biblical allusion. "Are you not your brother's keeper?"

"See what I mean," my sister said.

"I swanny," Mrs. Swope said, brushing a hand to her mouth, stifling a laugh.

"Don't get them started, Gayle," my mother warned. "Act like a pair of hyenas when they scrap."

The business day had officially begun, with the adults packed into conference rooms to study the Prophets or the Epistles, their children farmed out to a day camp supervised by counselors recruited from Samford and Wake Forest. "Sugar, take good care of Dollbaby. You're older, after all, and the boy," my mother said before she sent us off. "Both of y'all behave." Although technically not a Baptist, Marilyn had been enlisted as a counselor this year. In her fringe vest and dungarees, she escorted my sister and me across the entrance road and along a steep trail to the camp, a fifteen-minute hike into tawny grass-lands. The Glorieta groundskeepers had cleared a few acres and erected a cinder-block bathhouse, open-air shelters with picnic tables. Along with over a hundred other children, my sister and I crammed into one of these shelters, found seats among the redwood benches.

Marilyn passed around some construction paper and scis-sors and Magic Markers. I stole glimpses of the other children as they cut out their name tags. I was sitting opposite Tammy and Taffy, identical twins from Pennsylvania, slight girls with Dorothy Hamill bobs and horn-rimmed glasses. My sister had already been adopted by two precociously curvaceous seventh graders, both of whom wore ripped Levi's shorts, T-shirts air-brushed with *Bay City Rollers* and *Styx*. They pronounced my sister "adorable," let her rifle through their macramé purses, explaining the different eye shadows in their compacts. They told her she should call them Farrah and Jaclyn.

One camper—a lanky girl named Cathy with dark ringlets, about my age—had crawled onto another table. Marilyn repeatedly asked her to take her place on a bench. Another counselor, a Samford student with a scraggly goatee, gently pulled Cathy's arm, but she swatted away his hand. There was something wrong with her face; her eyes crossed, and spit dribbled from her mouth. She carried a wad of tissue, coughed when she spoke; a croupy cough, like a puppy's bark. Marilyn finally coaxed Cathy down with a Fig Newton, but not before the girl's behavior had preempted sing-along time. Already the other kids were snickering and pointing at her, egged on by Jaclyn and Farrah, who in less than two hours had established themselves as the reigning alpha females. Cathy seemed oblivious to the whispered insults, Kleenex Cathy and Retardo.

At the morning recess, I shared oatmeal cookies with Taffy and Tammy, the twins from Pennsylvania, while my sister wedged between Jaclyn and Farrah at one of the tables, holding her lips in a pout as Farrah applied some berry-flavored gloss.

"That blond girl is your sister?" Taffy said. "Looks like she's part of the 'in crowd.' "

"Don't get it," I said. "Ten-year-olds don't wear makeup. My mom would smack her."

"She's cute as a button," Tammy said.

Cathy was pushing a stick through the dust, jabbering to herself. While the other kids considered her irritating, an object of contempt, I saw a diamond in the rough. I vowed to look after her the way Brother Roy looked after our congregation, tend to her as my mother had tended to me. Taking care of the weakest and most vulnerable, even if it required a little personal sacrifice: wasn't that what Brother Roy had always taught us? Wasn't that the Baptist way?

"Hey, Taffy," I said, wiping away crumbs with the back of my hand. "Marilyn said we're gonna play kickball. Let's make sure we get Cathy on our team."

Taffy's eyes narrowed. "Why her? She walks funny. Bet she can't kick a ball worth a durn."

Taffy's comment—snide, condescending—reminded me of something. *None of us want him for a team.* I glanced over: several older guys now circled while Jaclyn dabbed blush across my sister's cheeks. Jocks, with basketball jerseys and puka-bead necklaces, the leader a fifteen-year-old named Steve, auburn hair parted down the middle, muscular shoulders, curls nestled in his armpits. I leaned in conspiratorially.

"Brother Roy would want us to. Remember that verse in the Bible: *as ye have done it unto one of the least of these my brethren, ye have done it unto me.*"

"Weird, man," Tammy said. "Where you from, again?"

"I think Jesus was talking about poor people, not some annoying dork like Cathy," Taffy said. "Who's Brother Roy?"

"Our pastor," I said, fomenting a plan. I would save Cathy, beloved of Jesus if scorned by kids like my sister. "You'll probably get to hear him preach a sermon later this week."

"I know what I'd like to do unto those bitches," Taffy said, eyeing Farrah and Jaclyn and stamping a tuft of sage.

"Hush your mouth, Taffy," Tammy said.

Marilyn brought over a plastic garbage bag, and we tossed in our cookie wrappers. She curtsied girlishly. Her mood suggested she was enjoying herself far more than she'd expected. She'd wound her hair into a disheveled bun, stray wisps falling into her face. "I have an announcement: *Brian* and *I*"—with her thumb and index finger she made a pistol, aimed it at the counselor from Samford—"are going to referee a kickball game before Bible study. We're choosing sides, y'all, so let's go!"

Most of the younger kids were deemed too small to play, so Marilyn organized them as cheering sections on either side of the makeshift playing field. I assumed Jaclyn and Farrah would sit out the game, perch snootily on a picnic bench and polish their toenails, but instead they allowed my sister to pull them to Steve's side. In fact, after the two teams had divvied up the pool of prospective players, they seemed grossly mismatched, with the older, glamorous kids facing . . . well, facing some nearsighted, prepubescent boys, including me, plus Tammy and Taffy. And Cathy.

"We're doomed," Taffy said. "Doomed, I say."

"We got Cathy, we got Cathy, woo-hoo!" I said, jumping on the strip of cardboard designating home plate. Cathy stared in my direction, eyes unfocused. Steve and his crew fanned out across the clearing, laughing and chewing gum, with Farrah poised on a rise of bare ground, holding a plastic ball. Tapped as her team's catcher, my sister walked over, her face caked with makeup.

"You look like a clown," I said.

She sniffed without looking at me. "You're a turkey," she said.

"What did you say?"

"A jive turkey," she said, squatting down to intercept Farrah's pitch.

"Up your nose with a rubber hose," I said.

Tammy managed a blunt kick toward left field, slid into first base, a bit of beginner's luck. She was followed by a weedy ten-year-old from Alabama, who popped one over Steve's head, scoring a double. Jaclyn was laughing so hard she dropped the ball, giving Tammy a chance to steal home. Steve ran into the infield, threw his arms flirtatiously around Tammy, and swung her in a circle.

As my team's self-appointed coach, I realized that we were being mocked. We were the meek, the poor in spirit, persecuted because of righteousness. We would inherit the earth—or at least this kickball game, if I had any say. At home plate for her turn, Cathy craned her head toward the pitcher's mound, dazed, not really grasping Farrah's role. From the outfield came a faint but distinct chant: *Re-tar-do, Re-tar-do . . .*

"Let me explain," Farrah said in a ringing voice. "I. Will. Pitch. The. Ball. To. You. And. You. Will. Kick. It."

"Girl, you're cracking me up," Jaclyn called out, holding her sides.

Farrah pitched the ball in a deliberate slow motion. Brows furrowed, Cathy studied it as it rolled toward her. For an instant she balanced on one leg like a flamingo as she drew back her other foot, aiming for the center of the ball, watched impassively as it arched above Steve's head and plummeted into the juniper draw that marked the camp's boundary. Tammy and Taffy and I whooped, "Run, run, *run!*" Cathy darted toward third base, taking three strides for every foot forward, limbs akimbo like a vaudevillian actor's. An outfielder retrieved the ball, which Steve pocketed in his hands, threw back to Farrah.

"She has to run the right way," Jaclyn said.

I felt a heat bleeding into my face, walked to third base, where Cathy was rocking back and forth on the balls of her feet, smiling so wide I could see her gums. "Cathy, we need to try again. You have to run to the right, to *first* base." She sneezed from an updraft of dust, followed me docilely back to home plate.

"All *right,* goobers," Farrah said, flicking back a sweep of blond hair. "Let's try this again." She shot a not-nice look at Jaclyn, glanced back over her shoulder at Steve, coconspirators in her subtle tyranny. The world saw a beautiful girl on the cusp of her teenage years, with porcelain features and burgeoning breasts, the moment in her life when calculated cruelty was expected, even cultivated; but I saw Medusa.

"We must defeat her," I shouted. "We must save Cathy the way Perseus saved Andromeda!"

"What?" Taffy said.

"Jive turkey," my sister said, crouching in the dust.

"All right, all right," Brian shouted from over my shoulder. "Put a sock in it and just play ball."

Farrah pitched again. Cathy kicked the ball toward the draw. As Steve chased after it, she ran toward first base in that loose-legged, inefficient way. Like a traffic cop, I pumped my arm, shouting, "That way, that way, go to second base, second *base.*" Cathy leapt over the two-by-four that served as first base and kept running in a straight line, a frantic vector through right field and past a clump of dwarf oaks and toward the slope of a low hill, sprinted gangly-limbed to the crest, and disappeared down the other side. Marilyn and Brian rushed after her, reaching the top of that first hill just as Cathy appeared on the next rise, diminished, like a girl spied through the wrong end of binoculars, moving awkwardly through the chaparral, shrinking to a stick figure even as the counselors gained on her, smaller and smaller, lost among the high grasses, past saving.

On our last evening in Glorieta, following the six o'clock supper in Texas Hall, we joined the droves of Baptists pouring into the mammoth sanctuary, its spire illuminated and reflected in a pond, a blur of gold in a wash of twilight blue. Brother Roy had been asked to give the closing sermon, a signal that he was being considered for a leading position at the national headquarters. We filed into pews that had been roped off near the front, a VIP section to honor his home congregation. I noticed a couple of older men in the empty choir loft, hunched over a tape recorder and wearing headphones like earmuffs, sorting through eight-track cassettes—Brother Roy's words would spread throughout the country, spores wafted to germinate his fame.

After the opening hymn, he approached the pulpit, sporting his trademark horn-rimmed glasses, silver hair slicked back. He leaned toward the microphone, asked the audience to please open their Bibles to Exodus. The passage highlighted the travails of the Hebrews after they'd crossed the Red Sea, as they journeyed through the Wilderness of Sinai, incurring Jehovah's wrath during the Golden Calf episode. These forty years of suffering were critical, Brother Roy intoned, a purification required before they could enter the Promised Land. A whole generation who'd labored as Pharaoh's slaves had to die off so that a younger, freer people could emerge.

"They had to be refined in the fires of adversity," he said, drawing out his sentences in high evangelist mode, silkily trilling key syllables—*reFINED in the FIRES of adVERSity*—and touching off a tremor along my neck. "They had to be polished to a radiance worthy of Jehovah Himself." A few *amen*s skittered like wavelets through the sanctuary.

He paused, aware that he owned the crowd. So often since his wife had died, back in the winter, he'd seemed wan, unsure of himself, his voice gruff with loss, but here, with the aid of a prominent pulpit, he'd recovered his former robust self. He trained his high-beam gaze through the cavernous room, letting it drift from the balcony to the aisles to our group at the front, resting finally on me. I felt the thrill of something about to happen—something adult and magnificent, in front of all those thousands of Baptists.

Then he asked me to stand.

I stood.

"Folks, that there is somebody." *SomeBODy.* "He knows, quite literally, what it means to polish something. Y'see, he owns a stone-polishing machine, one of those rubber drums that turns on a conveyor, back home in Tennessee. Just last week I gave him some pieces of jade I'd purchased in Turkey last year, beautiful pieces."

My own Promised Land opened before me: creeks nourished by mineral springs, hills frothy with bluebells and yarrow, meadows where the elect could romp and worship God as they basked in His celestial glow. It came into focus just beyond the tip of my nose, bit by bit, like a mosaic of lapis lazuli, carnelian, jade.

"Y'see, I'd hoped to hire a jeweler to fashion a ring for my dear wife, Beryl"—he inhaled audibly, the microphone catching a wetness in his throat—"sweet, sweet Beryl, who checked into her mansion in Glory last January. Now I'm thinking of a bracelet for our daughter, Kelly. She looks just like her mother.

Seventeen years old, my girl. Maybe I can bribe her to apply to colleges close to home." A few chortles from the audience. "Close to home, like all children should be, near their parents. Her father." A murmur of sympathy. "You parents know what I mean."

I was still standing. Hardly breathing.

"Right now I bet those pieces of jade are tumbling over and over in that polishing drum, those stones polished to a dazzling shine," he said. I nodded vigorously. "Yes, he's nodding, he's nodding . . . Can't wait to see my beautiful jade!"

He raised his left hand, cupped the air, motioning for me to sit. For the rest of the sermon, the crowd sat transfixed, bursting into applause when he finished off. The organist cranked up "It's a Happy Day." We all joined in, singing avidly, my mother straining for the high notes, my father's bullfrog bass.

Technically this was not an invitational hymn, as we were all presumably saved, but several older couples walked forward to rededicate their lives to Jesus, followed by a pair of weeping teenage girls. I squirmed forward to see if they were Jaclyn and Farrah, but they were both at least sixteen and heavier, not so pretty. Brother Roy stepped down from the dais, laid his hands on their quivering heads.

For a moment I considered going forward as well. But I'd already rededicated myself during the spring Revival—it had turned into an annual, attention-seeking ritual since I'd been saved four summers ago—and I could imagine my sister rolling her eyes.

I was humming as the congregation dispersed into the cool night to head back to Oklahoma Hall to pack, gliding on a current as light as vapor, as strong as bedrock. I passed Cathy with her parents and smiled at her, feeling a pang of vindication: this lost girl embodied some cosmic truth that my sister and Farrah and Jaclyn would never understand, let alone appreciate. But I knew, and so did God. And this secret wisdom would be a lamp unto my feet and a light unto my path, while my sister wallowed pathetically in the slough of her ignorance and vanity.

Cathy smiled back, a vacant expression on her asymmetrical face. I was ready to go home, cleansed and polished to an iridescence visible only to unseen eyes, but no less real.

The highway wound through a desert of wind-scoured boulders and sere hills, past stands of mesquite and ocotillo. Trailers lined the road's shoulder, advertising bottle rockets and Roman candles for sale. With the approach of evening, Mr. Draper parked the bus in the Carlsbad lot, where we disembarked to the hoots of owls roosting in junipers. Tomorrow we would tour the cave, but now we'd watch the famous bats of Carlsbad rouse from their slumber. Brother Roy had timed our arrival to the performance.

He'd found a place for all of us in the viewing amphitheater just outside the cave's yawning mouth, with its overhang of rock, speckled with guano, and the dark cavity that hinted at the rooms below. As dusk fell, the scouts flitted out, beating their wings and emitting high-pitched clicks. They circled for a moment, and then the space above the amphitheater was black with a column of bats, rotating like a tornado out of the earth as they flew toward their hunting grounds along the Pecos River, glimmering like smoke in the waning light.

"Outasight," Marilyn said, one arm slung around me and the other hugging my sister. "Rad."

The show had lasted about ten minutes. I glanced at my mother: her tongue prodded the inside of her mouth. Something about the bats had unnerved her. My father noticed as well. "Didn't you think that was great, honey? The kids loved it. Honey?"

She didn't answer.

Long after we were asleep in our beds at the Carlsbad Holiday Inn, the bats navigated the skies over the desert, Mexican free-tails and pipistrelles, clicking into the dark for prey.

The next morning I could tell that my mother's mood lingered. As we stood with other tourists outside Carlsbad's entrance, she withdrew from Mrs. Swope's gossip, kept taking her sunglasses on and off even after we'd passed through the turnstile. My father touched her arm, but she shrugged away his hand. He looked at me with a quizzical expression: *What can you do?*

The trail descended in switchbacks, like a burro's path. Each new bend dropped us deeper into twilight. I looked over my shoulder to see the cave's mouth dwindling to a pinpoint of sky. A wind rose from the depths, cooling our cheeks. The voices of tourists ahead of us echoed back in murmurs. All around us was the dank smell of earth and guano. The guide pointed down a pitch-black chamber that plunged away off to our left. "Folks, that's the main sleeping compartment of Carlsbad's bat community—we call it the Dracula Arms! Those critters sleep all day and hunt all night, mosquitoes, gnats. If you stick around until evening, you'll see 'em leave the cave. It's spectacular!"

In the dim light I could not see my mother's face.

The trail leveled near the bottom of the cave. I felt her hand on my neck, fingers rigid as pincers. She was breathing heavily. The group jostled against a railing, just outside the Big Room. Beneath a neon light, Brother Roy's face looked unnatural, a sallow moon. I heard the slap of my sister's sandals a few feet away.

"Honey, bat got your tongue?" my father joked.

My mother was silent. The guide previewed the wonders that lay ahead: Rock of Ages, the Totem Pole, Longfellows Bathtub. A light gleamed: a snack bar tucked into an alcove of stone. An aroma of buttered popcorn, the dyspeptic gush of a Slurpee machine. I sensed the bustle of an underground city, one with its own features and thoroughfares but also with hazards, camouflaged slabs, hidden sumps. A few steps from the trail and you'd slip through a crevasse and no one would know where you'd gone. You'd wander among the bats and limestone hollows, lost forever in a perpetual night.

Disoriented, I stepped forward, following the guide's voice. I felt light-headed at the thought of millions of cubic tons of rock piled above us, reached out to balance myself against my sister but grabbed only air. Was she lagging behind? She'd held Marilyn's hand on the descent, asking about clothes and shampoo and boyfriends, but now Marilyn shuffled ahead with her arm around her grandmother.

"My God!"

My mother's voice, half yowl, half curse. Her hand worked my neck like a saw. My palms went clammy. Down here I sensed the beginning of the end of the world.

"What's wrong?" my father said.

The snack bar's spectral light played across his face. Somehow my neck had caught beneath her bicep. "Where is she?" she said. "Where did Dollbaby go to?"

He funneled his hands around his mouth, called my sister's name. Again, louder.

"Folks, everything all right?" The guide stood before us in silhouette, hat in hand. My mother released her grip and shook her head as Mrs. Sanders wrapped her in an embrace. My father said that he'd last seen his daughter at the base of the trail, next to the emergency elevator doors. He waved his arms forward as though the cave had sucked her down, down to the center of the earth. The guide took notes—*dressed in a yellow T-shirt and blue jeans, uh-huh, blond ponytails like Cindy on* The Brady Bunch—and then steered my father into the crowded darkness. Some of our group had disappeared down the trail that dipped along the perimeter of the Big Room. I could see a glare of klieg lights trained on the first formations.

A verse from 1 Kings popped into my mind, calmed me. *Gird your loins.* I leaned into my mother, trying to feed my faith into her veins by osmosis, molecule by molecule. "Trust in the Lord," I said. "It will be all right."

"Jeannie, you go ahead," my mother said to Mrs. Sanders.

"Cholly, are you sure?"

"Lanny will find her. She's in a mess of trouble. I've done told her and told her not to run off. She's been impossible since she met those older girls. This morning I caught her trying to put on my lipstick."

Mrs. Swope and the Norways hesitated as my mother rubbed her hands together, a peal of anxious laughter.

"Y'all go ahead. A mess of trouble. She's gonna learn a thing or two about disobeying."

They started down the trail, uneasy, glancing back until they disappeared around the first turn. Suddenly my mother bent forward and jerked me to face her. Her voice was a growl, an octave lower than I'd heard before.

"Get me the hell out of here right now."

We walked to the emergency elevator, where I explained to a security guard that my sister was lost in Carlsbad Caverns, that my mother wasn't handling this news well, and that events had spiraled out of control and thus constituted an emergency. He beckoned us in, offered a sympathetic look as the door slammed shut. As we ascended, he mentioned that she could file a missing person's report with the park rangers. A neon light flickered in the car, carving my mother's nose and silent mouth into a grotesque mask. Then the door swung open: a glare blinded us as we stepped blinking into the spacious lobby of the visitors' center, with its beamed ceiling, Formica floor, and full windows that gave views of the Sonoran Desert and the Guadalupe Mountains.

She stared out at the arid peaks and hummocks, a garden of yucca and cactus in the foreground, the veins in her neck thin and defined, like a tree's twigs. I reached around her waist, let out a self-important sigh. My sister had run off like some smart-alecky, ungrateful girl, but I'd stayed right by our mother's side. Surely there was a metaphor in this. "I'd like to lead us in a prayer for her safe return," I said.

"Don't touch me," she said. "Don't ever touch me again."

But she let me hold her while I recited the Shepherd's Psalm. I even mimicked Brother Roy's lilt: *YEA, though I WALK though the VALley of the SHAdow of DEATH, I will FEAR no EVil.* After a while she fished her sunglasses from her purse, put them on, said to no one in particular, "The bats took her. Just carried her off." She'd slipped far beyond me, into a solitary cave of her own. I did not know what to do or to say.

She unhooked my arms. The elevator door opened again, and my father and Brother Roy walked forcefully across the lobby, my sister in tow, a sly grin on her face. Her sandals slid on the slick floor as she tried to match their stride. My mother noticed their reflection in the window's glass, turned around to feel my sister's shoulders. She inspected the knees and shins. There was a single scrape; my sister had taken a tumble when my father pounced on her, near the end of the loop around the Big Room.

"Snuck off without asking permission," my father said. "Thought she was being cute, I guess. Don't know what's gotten into her lately." He whistled through his teeth. "She apologized in the elevator."

My mother produced a Band-Aid from her purse, said softly, "Don't ever run off like that again. You absolutely scared me to death." Her relief reached her then, like the shock of delayed thunder; tears welled in her eyes, a grief deferred. Brother Roy patted her shoulder, eyes moist with empathy, as though this incident had triggered something that churned inside him, unbidden and largely unseen.

"We got her back, Cholly," he said. "We got her back safe and sound, praise the Lord."

My father snaked his hand around my mother's waist as she scooped up her daughter. Like an afterthought, I was pushed back against a rack of brochures advertising scenic attractions throughout the Southwest: "You'll Love Beautiful Historic Taos"; "This Year Vacation in the Only Town Named after a Television Show—Truth or Consequences, N.M.!" In that moment we struggled back toward a family equilibrium. Her humor restored, my mother planted a kiss on my father's cheek. They held hands as they followed Brother Roy through the center's front doors to reunite with the Sanderses and Mrs. Swope outside.

But an image persisted, growing in the dark, long after I'd fallen asleep in hotel rooms from Albuquerque to Oklahoma City to Little Rock, assembling itself methodically as the bus rolled into the church parking lot in Chattanooga, where I posed sunburnt with Marilyn in a snapshot, thanked Brother Roy for all of his spiritual direction, and promised that I'd bring the polished jade to a worship service soon. Deep in the Big Room, where my sister had scraped her knee, the skin cells regenerated, forming a hip, an arm, then chin and hair. Eventually a girl rose from the pavement, lithe and blond, but only for a moment as she skulked into the recesses away from the trail. Deprived of light and air, she rapidly aged to a crone, a cave woman with hair tatted around her pallid face, her dress hanging in shreds.

I imagine she lives there still, exiled by her dread of those tourists gaping at the gypsum beds and Temple of the Sun. She prefers the anonymous chambers, unknown to even the most ardent spelunkers and away from the guides and crowds, that welter of humanity nursing their private pains, rebellious daughters and bewildered sons, grieving husbands and terrified mothers. She remembers her clone like a figure from a dream, that twin sister who now sits upright in her pew each Sunday, lips pinched and eyes emptied of warmth, the one who hectors her brother—*you're barking up the wrong tree with embryonic stem cell research*—even as he wants to rescue the lost, irreverent girl, her impish grin, her wisecracks at his expense. The cave woman shudders at how all those resentments have built up their tectonic layers over the years, smothering forgiveness beneath an impregnable crust.

Now she paddles a skiff down a subterranean river, searching for some jagged path up to a world she's never seen. And when she tires, an exhaustion that seeps into her bones, she clambers into her grotto, where she buries her sorrow among tiers of stalactites and stalagmites, beneath piles of polished gems, her callused hands tracing a sheen of obsidian and agate and amethyst.

6

VICTORY

"What is it about your people and victory?" Ellen asks. "What do you mean?"

"You know, *victory*. That word comes up a lot. The concept."

Tonight she's made curried vegetables for dinner, chickpeas and broccoli florets over basmati rice, spooned into ceramic bowls. We've carried a couple of chairs and glasses of seltzer into Owen's room, joking about a movable feast. Outside sleet laminates the sycamores angled against the façade of our apartment building, the cape jessamine vine withered to a thread. A gloom socks in Brooklyn, early dusk, Thanksgiving less than two weeks away.

At the age of fourteen months, after a seven-month stay at Columbia Presbyterian, Owen had rebounded enough to discharge home. In the intervening months, we've labored to master his knotty health-care regimen, his menu of medications. I've learned to siphon a catheter down his throat, watching him gag as I suction out the froth that puddles in his lungs, worse when he's got a virus. We've already gone though a succession of part-time nurses, ranging from the competent to the barely aware, but mostly we manage his exhausting care ourselves, complicated by Ellen's pregnancy. She's three months along with twins, hobbled by fatigue, her Rockette legs knock-kneed with her burgeoning weight.

She'd spent her childhood in a Volvo, shuttling along the maze of Los Angeles's freeways, up and down canyons and coulees, her early life sieved through a mesh of smog and Less Than Zero anomie. The daughter of academic parents, imports from New York, she'd grown up with heated political debates around the dinner table, vile-Nixon-this, jerk-Reagan-that; cello lessons; screenings of films by Kurosawa and Herzog. Summers in Copenhagen and London, where her father would lecture on his areas of expertise, schizophrenia and bipolar disorder.

In Los Angeles she'd always felt a little schizophrenic herself, disconnected from the city that sprawled around her; from blond, silicone-enhanced actresses strutting the Sunset Strip, gangs clashing along Venice's Boardwalk, Manson-look-alike panhandlers on Hollywood Boulevard. A kaleidoscope of palm trees and traffic lights and strip malls and dirty air, shadows engraving Mulholland's gated drives, bleached by an arid light. Hills iridescent with eucalyptus trees, yucca fronds sharp enough to cut your hand. The years at a private girls' school had seemed oppressive. She'd half-applied herself, scraping by in algebra and chemistry but earning high marks in history and her women's studies elective. Afternoons she'd lick stamps as a volunteer in the office of her congressman, run out for coffee for her boss, pick up the phone during the lunch break. She'd harbored ambitions to work in local government someday, or as an urban planner, maybe in her shining nirvana, New York. That she'd accomplished her goals spoke to the persistence that glittered in her green eyes.

Now two years old, Owen slumps in his crib, buttressed by pillows, breathing and feeding tubes webbed over his shoulders. Lately we've eaten our dinner here, on either side of him, hashing the day's highs and lows. Our conversations seem to comfort him, lull him to sleep, even if the topic of debate raises our voices and blood pressure, such as a just-held, contentious presidential election.

"That article in the *Times* today, oy," Ellen says, a prissy pat of a cloth napkin to her mouth. "They're calling it a victory for the 'values voters,' whatever that means." The photographs accompanying the story had shown various name-brand clergy smiling and shaking hands. White men with blow-wave haircuts, piggy faces. "As if those of us who don't vote their way lack values." She swallows a bite, sips her seltzer, lumbers to her feet, a firmness to her belly. Her hair glossy, bathed in a cream of hormones. She ferries her bowl back to the kitchen. I hear it clatter in the sink, the refrigerator door swing open as she rifles through Owen's bottles of medication.

I chew slowly. My mouth simmers with the cumin and cayenne she threw into the skillet. She's unwittingly touched on the core of the evangelical ethos: manic desire to win. All acts of charity and faith flagged in the face of this vicious, almost gladiatorial, sense of competition. Like Bible Drill in fifth grade, when I almost—*almost*—soared to Olympian heights.

"Y'all let me tell you what," my mother said. "I know what song I want played at my funeral." She tipped her chin back, eyes glistening, lips a cupid's bow: a Garbo face. She waited for us to clamor a response.

She waited.

And waited.

She glanced sidewise at my father, still belted in the driver's seat.

"What, Cholly?" my father said. "What song do you want played at your funeral?"

"Listen up, let me tell y'all," she said, "It's 'Victory in Jesus.' " She sang from the diaphragm in a scratchy baritone, deeper than any other mother's voice. She sang from a place of passion and certainty, convinced that when the appointed hour came she could still stage-manage from the Hereafter.

> *O victory in Jesus*
> *My Savior, forever.*

"Cut that out," my father said.

"Just trying to get into the spirit of Revival," my mother said.

We were sitting in the station wagon in the church parking lot, waiting for Revival service to begin, promptly at seven o'clock. A thunderstorm had bowled through the city that afternoon, snapping power lines and flooding the bogs and graveled lots along Chickamauga Creek, leaving behind a pristine May evening, an indigo sky bleeding its light. A few congregants had already climbed out of their Chryslers and Monte Carlos and had wandered toward the sanctuary, waving and calling out to my parents. My father had rolled down his window to answer, trading deacon gossip with Mr. Sanders and Mr. Allison. A scent of marigolds floated in from the lawns down Mayfair Avenue.

"Save it for worship service," he said, unlatching the belt's buckle and creaking open his door.

Our congregation was moving through an uneasy transition. Brother Roy had accepted a position at the national headquarters, bequeathing his storied stewardship of our congregation to a search committee of elders, including my father, tasked with pinpointing a successor. They'd pored over dossiers, traveled afield to South Carolina and Alabama and the ring of suburbs outside Atlanta to hear candidates preach, assessing each man's evangelical style. After a grueling process, they'd ended up with their default man, Brother Virgil, tall and portly, with a pasty face and Sansabelt pants. The congregation hadn't really warmed to him, but he'd been there for only a few months. "We got to give him a chance," my father had said, but I knew he was worried that Brother Virgil might not pan out, that we'd all drift about aimlessly, fertile soil for the devil's schemes.

My mother shared his concern. "An idle mind is the devil's workshop," she'd say. "Eyes on the prize." As an elder's wife, she was supposed to refrain from too many expressed opinions, let the men tend to the process. She wanted to contribute, though, help to train a fresh generation of leaders. Inevitably her attention locked on me. She charted a trajectory out loud. I'd demonstrated a proficiency with words. I could preach to the masses, change the world, it was possible. A missionary, broadcasting the Gospel.

She decided that Bible Drill would provide a solid foundation for my future career. On Sunday evenings, I'd sit in the sanctuary with my peers, hunched over the study guides issued by the Southern Baptist Convention. I'd recite in order the Bible's sixty-six books, Genesis through Revelation, memorize key scriptures like the Shepherd's Psalm and the Great

Commission, identify obscure characters such as Sisera and Ahab and James the Less.

The drill was structured in five parts and would last thirty pressurized minutes. Like in a popular television quiz show—*Match Game* or *Jeopardy!*—the questions moved from relatively simple to complex and densely theological. The practice sessions ground through humid Sunday evenings as we prepared for the three drills, Church, Association, and State. Three rounds of increasingly difficult competition.

The Church Drill was held informally, in a room off the Fellowship Hall, one with cork bulletin boards and an American flag in the corner. Before a half-circle of folding chairs, a line of tense children clasped their Bibles at their right sides, left sides for the left-handed participants. Mrs. Norway called the drill. She stood at a podium directly in front of us, composed in her polyester sundress, hair crimped into a bun. My mother had volunteered to serve as timekeeper.

Mrs. Norway instructed us on the drill's protocol, then launched into its first phase: Books of the Bible. "Present swords," she said, alluding to a verse of Saint Paul's that describes the Bible as the "Sword of the Spirit." I lifted my Bible into position, cover down, in front of my chest.

"Proverbs: begin."

Within ten seconds I had to find Proverbs, tap my finger to a verse, balance the book in my open palm, and step forward. I heard my mother call time. From my peripheral vision I discerned that the line of children had moved forward, intact, clearing the drill's first hurdle. Mrs. Norway said my name.

"Psalms, Proverbs, Ecclesiastes," I said, giving the names of the books preceding and following Proverbs. She nodded, and we all stepped back into formation.

"Hebrews: begin."

Hebrews, let's see, near the back, just before the two Peters and the three Johns. I turned directly to it, swaggered forward, my index finger brushing the page. This time Mrs. Norway called on Mandy Welch.

"Philemon, Hebrews, James."

The drill's second phase was more complicated: we had to search for a specific verse, again within the ten-second limit. My fingers tickled the onionskin pages. John 3:16—"For God so loved the world." Psalm 100:1—"Make a joyful noise." 1 Corinthians 13:13—"But the greatest of these is charity." There were casualties now, as a few of my colleagues—Mitch Fulghum and Dannette Parsons—wavered. I was still scoring a perfect game, maintaining my stride into the challenging memorization phase.

"At ease," Mrs. Norway finally said, wiggling a finger beneath her bun, scratching her ear. An air of relief was palpable in the warm room. I looked at my mother now where she sat on a piano bench, clutching the stopwatch, eyes lidded. A few minutes later one of the judges handed a list of the night's winners to Mrs. Norway, who read the results aloud: nine of the twelve participants had passed the Church Drill and would proceed to the County Association Drill, to be held the next Sunday at East Ridge Baptist Church.

The Association Drill was widely considered to be an intermediate stage, a numbers game, one that winnowed out the pretenders from the Right Stuff. That Sunday night I once again turned in a perfect performance, although a couple of my key Scripture searches—the Parable of the Sower and the Rapture of Elijah—were a bit rusty. Generally, I was better on the Old Testament. All those plagues and prophets and sinning kings captured my imagination in a way that Paul's didactic Epistles failed to do. The parting of the Red Sea, Saul's feud with David, the cosmopolitan court of Solomon—these were heady stories.

Now I was the county's leading candidate to win the State Drill the following month. When I received the association's gold-leafed certificate, I crossed the dais to shake the drill superintendent's hand, a twelve-year-old politician in a powder blue leisure suit, relishing my moment in the public eye. I could sense the difference at church: the approving smiles of my mother's friends, nods from the deacons, a personal mention from Brother Virgil himself at the close of the evening service.

On the Saturday morning before the State Drill, Craig Allison called to ask if I wanted to meet up at Holiday Bowl on Brainerd Road for a game or two. I picked up the wall extension in the den, caught the receiver beneath my chin as I coiled the cord around my wrist like a riding crop, suitable for flogging my soul. "Gotta bone up on these memorizations," I said.

"That's just plain dorky, period," he said, inserting a clumsy pause, his signature technique, a cobra's venom silently gutting any resistance, crippling its prey. I could hear other voices, a man and woman cursing each other. "Must be some kind of party line," I said.

"What do you honestly expect to get out of Bible Drill?" Craig said.

"Well, I think I'll be better at witnessing someday," I said. "Leading folks to the Lord."

A *humph* of disdain. "Are you in or do I have to call Tad?" Craig said. "Doody or get off the john."

My father agreed to drop me off after his lunch break. Set back in a parking lot forested with klieg lights, Holiday Bowl attracted kids from a spectrum of races and classes and neighborhoods, Alton Park and Hixson and Missionary Ridge. On the curb outside, students from Tennessee Temple, the fundamentalist school, milled around like storks, witnessing to the unclean. They stuck out in their starched shirts and black polyester slacks, skinny ties with vintage clips. The girls wore linen below-the-knee skirts, cambric blouses. We knew they looked down on the Southern Baptists as too liberal, too enamored of the fallen world, its movies and mass-market paperbacks and penny-dreadful entertainments.

Inside Holiday Bowl, Craig and I meandered among thirty alleys buffed to a blond luster. The overhead projectors tallied strikes and spares; bowling balls spat out by the automated chutes and clinked together like oversize pearls on a grooved track. We paid our five-dollar fee and laced up our shoes, soles scuffing the deck. I chose a ball the color of onyx. He wriggled his fingers into a marbled ball, wound his reedy arm, and let fly a Brooklyn, leveling the tenpins. He took an early lead, with two strikes and a spare, as my efforts bottomed in the gutters more often than not.

Over in the next alley, some black kids were goofing around, waddling up to the foul line and rocking the ball like an infant in a swing, chucking it forward granny-style to hoots of "Dion, thass outasight!" They'd smuggled in a transistor radio set to the local funk station, Bootsy Collins, George Clinton. I stepped off the deck and glanced down at Craig, who was marking up the card with a felt-tip pen.

"Dang, you suck," he said.

I ahemed to get his attention. He was studying the score. "Gonna lose this frame, mister," he said. "But here's what I'm gonna do: double or nothing, loser buys Cokes."

I coughed again. He looked up. "What?" he said.

I cut my eyes toward the black kids. "Think we better go witness," I said.

"No way," he said. "I hate witnessing."

"We gotta," I said. "Think how proud Brother Virgil would be."

"Let's stick with the game, ai-ite?"

He stuck the pencil behind his left jug ear, uncrossed a leg. A bowling ball slalomed into our lane, provoking laughter.

"Lord have mercy, Rico," one of the black kids said. He walked over to retrieve the ball, swallowed up by bell-bottom jeans and a fluorescent striped shirt, a denim cap muzzling his Afro.

"Great move," I called out. "Ha, ha. Have you heard about the Gospel of Jesus?"

Dion swiveled in slow motion to face me. I'd seen Jimmie Walker do the exact same move on *Good Times*.

"Get back here, Dion," Rico said.

"I go to church," Dion said, his eyes marbles of suspicion. "With my momma."

"Lots of folks go to church," I said, swelling up with bravado. The Lord had practically handed me a scalp for my belt. "But I ask you: just how many have really, really heard the Gospel of the Lord Jesus Christ?"

Dion's friends erupted in derisive laughter. He sniggered, turned away. Craig belched. From the far end of the alley came a *bonk-bonk,* balls connecting with pins, whoops of congratulations.

I stamped my foot on the foul line. "This means a lot to my future."

Craig glanced over at the next lane. The black kids were pointing at us. One yelled "Jesus boy," and they all laughed and hunched over, holding their sides as though pained. Evidently I'd disrupted their game. Craig laced his fingers together and cradled his face in their hammock, murmured, "Oh. My. Lord."

"Brother Virgil would want us to," I said. "You know the verse from Matthew: 'Go ye therefore, and teach all nations, baptizing them in the name of the Father, and of the Son, and of the Hoy Ghost.' "

Craig shook his head. "Shhuupperdorrk," he said, his voice muffled through his hands, despairing. More jeers and catcalls.

"I need the experience. I want to be a missionary."

Craig lowered his hands, rolled his eyes heavenward. And the Lord granted his silent prayer. One of the teenagers from Tennessee Temple, identifiable by his crew cut and monochromatic attire, had ventured inside to proselytize. He was sweating through his shirt, patches stuck to doughy skin. He waved to the black kids, offered a perky hello, dug in his pocket for a piece of twine, which he coiled between his thumb and index finger. "Let me show you a fun trick!" he said, loud enough for Craig and me to hear. "Think of this string as the Road of Life. And you're just going along, not really unhappy but maybe a little confused. What does it all mean?" He looped the twine around his pinkie, tugged it tight.

"Another soul brother," Rico announced to his friends.

"Got 'em on both sides," Dion said.

The proselytizer dropped his thumb, whiffled his hand like

a pretend bird, creating a twine cross that zigzagged across his open palm. He smiled widely, displaying a missing incisor.

"Time to split," Rico said.

They deposited the bowling balls on the storage rack, stripped off their shoes, cracking jokes about jive-turkey white boys. In less than a minute they'd swaggered out the entrance. Undaunted, the Temple guy slunk toward another lane, struck up a conversation with a couple of teenage girls.

I picked up my ball, inserted my fingers in its holes, felt them loose around my knuckles, like my father's college rings. Craig glowered his annoyance. "One of the dumbest things I've ever seen."

"Supposed to witness," I said. "That's what I'm learning in Bible Drill."

"Have you thought about a different career?"

For a moment I studied the lane, lining up my shot, then hurled my ball. It careened a path to the left and arced back, smashing into the one pin, knocking its siblings down in a domino effect. "Steeeerriiiiiiike!" Craig called. *That'll show him,* I thought. As far as I was concerned, the Road of Life arrowed in one true direction, deflected by nothing so meaningless as jibes and taunts, aiming toward a bull's-eye of evangelical accomplishment. And Bible Drill would help me get there.

On the appointed Sunday, with thunderheads pillared over the Cumberland Plateau, the station wagon cruised northward on I-75. The State Drill, the big time. My mother lectured me kindly but critically, a Southern Mama Rose, her voice lifted over the sweep of the windshield wipers.

"You have to be more aggressive, Sugar, get the job done in eight seconds so you don't cut it too close for comfort. You're sagging on those Scripture searches." As we neared the Sweetwater exit, she asked the eleventh-hour, preparatory questions.

"Okay, how about Micah?"

"Jonah, Micah, Nahum."

"How about Romans?"

"Acts, Romans, First Corinthians."

After we parked in the pebbled lot at Sweetwater Baptist Church, my mother led us through the church's double doors, my sister pressing the buttons on an electronic football game while I used the pamphlet to cram. We found the woman who would call the drill. Fifteen minutes later I stood at the end of a jittery line of children from all over the state, girls in ankle-length velvet dresses, boys in acrylic three-piece suits, all light-headed in the heat. A deacon had wedged open the doors, hoping to lure a breeze into the sanctuary.

"Present swords," a serene voice said.

My mother was stationed in the front pew, one leg crossed over the other, the stopwatch in her right hand. From the corner of my eye I could see her pink thonged sandals, her coral lipstick. She pressed her left hand down on my sister's electronic game when it bleeped, confiscating it.

"Judges."

At first the drill came off as easily as the earlier ones. I chewed my lip through the Scripture search, the First Miracle and the Promise to Abraham, and then . . . and then I heard in that even, detached tone the name of the one passage I couldn't identify.

"The Massacre of the Innocents."

Sounded very Old Testament to me, with its connotations

of blood and war and a punitive God, and I thumbed through the Samuels and the Kings, hoping for a signpost, a blip on my internal radar . . . no, nothing . . . five seconds, six . . . a spasm ricocheted through my legs as I remembered the original Innocent, Jesus Himself, saw in an instant of clarity and horror my mistake: how could I confuse the New with the Old? My fingers scurried past the minor Prophets and into the Gospels, please let it be Matthew, please . . .

"Time," my mother said.

I glanced up, my innocence massacred by that one word, a monosyllable that revealed the futility of all my promise and training. Time: irreversible, venal, final. My mother still dangled one leg over the other. She clasped my sister's electronic game with one hand and held the stopwatch in the other, away from her vest, as though it were a dead rodent.

There was a thirty-minute break before the awards ceremony. I rushed out the rear doors to the parking lot, where I found Tad and Craig squatting behind the fenders of a clay-flecked Oldsmobile, playing with a Bic lighter and a crushed pack of menthol Kools. They were flinging lit cigarettes into the goldenrod along the lot's curb, a made-up game with an obscure scoring system, joking about Smokey the Bear. The air reeked of honeysuckle cut by tobacco and exhaust from the highway.

"Streeeeerrrriiiike," Craig said.

A boom of thunder like a kettledrum, miles off. My shadow blotted their faces as they looked up. They'd stripped off their jackets and looped their ties around their foreheads like bandannas. The heat settled its layers over us, sapping our breath.

"Look it who's here," Tad said. "Mr. State Winner Perfect."

This summer he'd shot up five inches, arms plump with

muscle and voice deeper, a fuzz along his upper lip. He was in a position now to challenge Craig's supremacy over our clique but seemed content to hang back, share the power in a relatively peaceful alliance. Craig still spoke in his Mickey Mouse squeak, but he spoke assertively, as though he'd already preceded Tad across the Rubicon of puberty.

"Not this time," I said, feeling the sting of tears behind my eyes. "Gotta get my mind off it." I hunkered down next to them. "What'chall playing?"

"It's called 'The Solar System,' " Tad said.

Craig waved a cigarette close to his thigh. He let out a fart, craned to see if it had any effect on the ember, snickered at his own sulfurous wind. "Clouds of methane and ammonia surround Uranus," he said.

"The smeller's the feller," Tad said. He farted in solidarity. "Must be them *frijoles* from Taco Hell." He lit the end of another Kool, this one ripped, secreting wisps of tobacco. He tossed it to the curb. The cigarette flared and chewed itself down to the filter.

"What do you mean, you don't think you won?" Craig said. "You always win everything this stupid church throws at us."

From behind came a buzz of conversation. I glanced over my shoulder. Adults and children alike were dallying outside the sanctuary, restless in the steamy air, polyester clothes puckered along sticky skin. One nervous boy was jabbing a jackknife at the wall's spackling. My mother's harried face appeared in the porthole window of one of the doors, a planet transiting the sun, both hemispheres dark. Portents everywhere.

"Not today," I said. "Just let everybody down. Especially myself."

"Serves you right, embarrassing me at the bowling alley, all that witnessing crap."

"Man, I bombed," Tad said. "Even missed one of the Gospels, Luke. How about you, Craig?"

Craig whistled through his teeth. "Messed up the memorization, duh," he said. "But who cares? Seriously."

"I care," I said. "I really, really do."

He shook the Kool packet for the last cigarette, touched the Bic to its end. I stood, wiped my sweaty hands on my trousers, stunned by the fissure that had opened between two virtually identical Baptist boys. In a moment we'd march back into the Sweetwater sanctuary, back into the arena of our mutual failure, fuming (in my case) as Mandy Welch collected her accolade and the unspoken honorific of Most Outstanding Baptist Child. Little bits and pieces of me would perish, but Craig would only shrug, his skin armored against the superego that lay siege to us hourly, like Roman legions. We'd fend our way back to the familiar macadam that ran through the heart of our lives; and we'd begin to part, moving in opposite directions. This much I knew: one of us would make it out intact, his head more or less the same.

Which one?

Later, on the drive back to Chattanooga, as fat drops ticked across the windshield, my mother said, "My, my, the Massacre of the Innocents. It's practically a part of the Christmas story!"

She glared at me through the rearview mirror, and I slumped down in the backseat, feeling the crush of her chagrin. If I, her A student, couldn't serve as her apostle to the world, bipedal proof that she'd walked the earth, yearned for better things, and swallowed disappointments, then what good was I? Bible Drill was supposed to shepherd me in the proper direction, toward Speakers' Tournament, Youth Week Pastor, a seminary, and eventually an African country where emaciated women with their sickly infants would turn hollowed-out eyes to me, grateful for the rice bowls and spiritual sustenance that only I could provide.

But for now I'd come off the rails and needed to find another way back into the Lord's army. The larger cosmic struggle would play out, with only sporadic lulls, until the Second Coming, when we'd claim victory. A war of the ages, as broad and boiling as a galaxy but intimate and revelatory as well, a common object you could hold in your hand.

Present swords.

7

PLANT PAIN

A woman's hunger grows differently than a man's, stabbing its taproot through topsoil, seeking nutrients. It takes the long view, follows it own arc. Ten years, twenty, twenty-five: it organizes the space around it, hefty, an oak that anchors a lawn, shading neighborhood children as they play Kick the Can, elderly couples who set up card tables for cribbage and beakers of lemonade. The newspaper events line up, a string of birth and wedding announcements, obituaries, and still it exerts its authority. Not so with a man's desire, flaring up like fireweed to ravage a landscape, then smoldering out, ready for the rake.

My mother was tossing out the dead irises. She'd inspected the limp petals, the withered stalks, snapping their necks in two, decapitating them. "Sugar," she'd said, "bring me those pruning shears, you hear?" She'd bundled the remains and pitched them into the garbage can, lidded it like a sarcophagus, stems crushed, crawling with ants. I'd carried the can to the end of the driveway.

The heat funneled down from the Cumberland Plateau like a sirocco. My father—pink-faced, shirtless, perspiring—jockeyed the lawn mower across the front yard. I could hear him groan with effort. He'd done about half, neat ribbons of green where my sister now practiced her twirling routines. She yelled "Shootfire!" each time the baton wobbled free from her grip. My mother had bought her a tennis skirt and a pair of used ballerina slippers; she'd already stained them with grass juice and honeysuckle nectar.

My mother frowned as she worked her hoe along the azalea bed. "Just no natural-born gardener," she said. "Can't tell the difference between an annual and a perennial." She was obsessed with sprucing up her front yard, roses and irises, impatiens drizzled from the front door to the mailbox. She'd toyed with orchids in planters. Each year she sacrificed entire Saturdays to sprinklers and trowels and powdery fertilizers, with mediocre results.

In this regard she'd failed to live up to her own mother's high standard. My grandparents owned a peanut farm in South Georgia, where my mother had been raised, their acreage on the outskirts of a drowsy town cobbled together by a silver-domed courthouse, plate-glass storefronts and a Dairy Queen, silos brimming with soybeans and rye. It always seemed to be hot afternoon there, air shimmering over asphalt. Each spring my grandmother devoted herself to her craft, calling forth a blaze of zinnias and begonias and pansies, irises sturdy as sequoias. Her yard was the sole expression of a rich inner life. My mother had left this all behind her when she married, traded the country for the city, the sober Methodist customs for theatrical Baptist flourishes, embraced a definition of womanhood far removed from her mother's. No rural ways for her, no sirree bob. And yet part of her yearned to grow a rose so opulent that our neighbors would shower her with compliments.

Now she was leaning against her chaise as she sheafed the

dead roses, careful to avoid the thorns. "Plants don't feel pain, not like a dog or a cat," she muttered.

My father had pushed the lawn mower into the garage, switched it off. Sweat greased his belly fat. "Am I ever sore," he said. "I'll get the rest after lunch. And by the way: what is she doing?" He hitched a thumb toward my sister as she flipped the baton over her wrist, whacking her shoulder.

"Golly Miss Molly!" she said.

"Practicing for Twirl Day," my mother said.

My father rolled his eyes. For months he'd heard my mother's scheme. She was plotting something unusual for my sister, a secular pursuit that still fit within the box of our religious lives. An avocation that would yield benefits down the road, perhaps a scholarship to a desirable state university, a leg up in the charm and poise departments.

Majorette.

"Too hot for that silliness," my father said. "We got any Lipton?"

She reached behind the chaise and lifted a pitcher of tea, striped with moisture, ice cubes tinkling the sides.

"Oooo-wheee," he said. "Let me fetch a glass." He lumbered toward the front porch, rubbing an elbow with the opposite hand, banged the door shut behind him.

"How do you know?" I said.

"Know what?" my mother said, wiping her forehead with a kerchief.

"Just because plants don't talk don't mean they don't feel pain."

She looped the kerchief around her wrist. "Can you believe this heat?" Already she'd started on a tan, her skin the tint of mocha, a whiff of cocoa butter. She stepped back a pace to size me up. "Sugar, maybe you should spend less time worrying about dead flowers, more time worrying about your grammar." There was a raspy edge to her voice. We'd come to this: all my straight A's and high praise from Brother Roy and the other elders at church, none of it elevated me in her eyes, or in my father's. Since I'd choked last year in the State Bible Drill, she'd made it clear I was something of a disappointment. Part of me wondered why I even bothered.

I walked the roses down to the garbage can, stuffed them in a layer above the irises, their thorns like warts, stems gnawed through by aphids.

My mother had enrolled my sister at the Tennessee Academy of Majorettes, known by its acronym, TAM. Each Tuesday, after school, my sister would line up with other eleven-year-olds in the gym of All Saints Academy downtown, training baton in hand, to learn the basics of twirling, strutting, and parade formation. TAM's director—a leggy young woman named Donna, who favored velour jumpsuits—rode herd on the girls. While a portable phonograph scratched out John Philip Sousa, she barked orders: *Chin up, Missy . . . Don't let that baton touch the floor, Kayla.* My mother watched from the bottom row of the gym's bleachers, her hand patting time on her knee.

Occasionally I tagged along. As I sat next to my mother, a shaft of sunlight would beam down from the gym's high windows, casting an aura on the most important alumna in TAM's ten-year history: Starla Scruggs, sixteen years old, now head majorette at Central High and the reigning queen of twirling tournaments and beauty pageants throughout a three-state re-gion. Starla served as Donna's number two and a role model for my sister's class, coaching them on the technique of finger control. She was tall for her age, with a satiny braid of dark hair down her back, eyes like chips of amethyst, and skin the texture of porcelain. When she whirled her baton into the air, I noticed the muscular flex of her thighs.

Starla Scruggs—former Miss Petite Southeast Tennessee, for-mer Photogenic Princess, current Senior Miss Southeast Tennes-see, and the odds-on favorite to win next year's Miss Chattanooga title—Starla Scruggs suffered from one disability, a flaw that did not mar her china-doll complexion but rather affected her voice, her sense of timing on the gym floor.

She wore hearing aids in both ears.

I'd never been around someone with a disability before, with the exceptions of Cathy, the girl whose cause I'd championed at Glorieta, and Twila Norway at church, whose bone disease re-quired bulky braces, the occasional use of a wheelchair. Twila taught a children's Sunday School class, played in the hand-bell choir, drove her own car, its gearshift and steering wheel adapted for her. Mrs. Sanders and my mother ahhed and oohed over Twila, talked about what an inspiration she was, that pre-cious girl.

I was ahhing and oohing over Starla. Years of rigorous prac-tice had enabled her to transcend the limitations of near-total deafness. She never dropped the baton midroutine, counting to herself even though she couldn't hear the music. That I con-sented to spend Tuesdays at the All Saints' gym, with its hot-house dankness, watching the Kimberleys and Brandis trip on their batons, enduring hours of ennui as my sister apprenticed herself to a profession, was a testament to the striking beauty and nimble grace of Starla Scruggs, older, captivating woman, princess of my imagination.

The last Saturday in June would be the climax of all that hard work: Twirl Day, when the TAM girls would wriggle into sequined leotards, curl and Dippity-Do their hair, primed to compete against the students of Tennessee Twirling Institute and the Chattanooga Charm Squad. The competition would last until late in the afternoon, as legions of twirlers vied for baroque, outsize trophies, engraved with WEE MISS CONGE-NIAL and PAGEANT BEST ALL-AROUND. Donna was nervous; she confided to my mother that she secretly hoped to poach some promising talent from T.T.I. and the Squad. As a last-minute schedule change, she penciled in a cameo appearance by Starla, a twirling solo that would kick off the pageant.

That morning we arrived at All Saints, and my mother hustled my sister out of the car, fussing with her pink foam curlers. I drifted along in their wake. Just inside the gym's lobby, next to the Coke machine, I spied Starla . . . but a Starla transfigured, sheathed in a leotard of black and gold sequins, a cape of nylon. She had already made up her face, wound her hair into a bun. She wore a tiny coronet of fake seed pearls and carried her baton like a scepter.

O Starla, queen of those first, preadolescent yearnings, sealed off in memory like a gorgeous bee in amber.

My mother prodded my sister toward the pack of girls in the middle of the gym. The lights dimmed, cuing the girls to sit cross-legged on the floor, flushing the mothers into the bleachers, loud whispers thrown over the shoulders: *Good luck, Shannon . . . You're a winner, Brittany, Momma loves you!* I found my mother in her customary place in the bleachers, my sister's contest leotard draped delicately across her lap like a veil of expensive lace. Her hands worried the leotard's zipper, its elastic cuffs.

"What's Starla gonna do? I saw her by—"

"Oh, hush up, Sugar," she hissed. "Don't bother me."

Minutes later Starla herself answered my question when she strode into the gym with the smile and gait of a celebrity come home to her old neighborhood. Before the huddle of girls, she flourished the baton, held the pose as the music began, cheered on by a few nine-year-olds who called themselves the Double-S Club. And then I saw Starla in her element, Starla as a kinetic verb—sucking in a breath, I beheld the consummate artistry of Starla Scruggs. The slender arms wove from side to side; the baton blurred from hand to hand; the gold sequins dazzled.

I glanced at my mother. "Starla, you dreamboat," she murmured, her eyes slits of gratitude. "You lovely girl, you doll-baby."

The music was building to a crescendo. Starla's shoulders bobbed furiously, the baton a glint at her side. She hurled it toward the gym's steel rafters in a series of exquisite revolutions. The baton gyred up and then yielded to gravity, spinning as it plummeted, aiming for Starla's outstretched palm. And then . . . and then the baton slipped through her fingers, slammed into the floor with a *thwack,* startling all the girls and mothers, Starla most of all. I wanted to yell *Just pick it up and go on,* but one unruly synapse shouted that it was all over, that Starla's disciplined rise to stardom had reached its apogee, like the baton, and would slant downward from this moment, forever.

She picked up the baton and resumed the routine, that sweet, enraptured smile painted across her face. The music halted, and I could hear the *click-click* of the phonograph's needle. She twirled and danced through the final measures, unaware of the silence, mouthing *two-three-four, two-three-four,* and then she triumphantly waved her hands above her head. For a stunned moment there was no noise. Then Donna switched off the phonograph.

Silence, lasting a beat, two, three, four. The entire gym seemed to pivot around the fulcrum of Starla's glorious, painful moment.

I flinched as my mother clapped, a *pop-pop-pop* that echoed until it was joined by the sound of all the other mothers clapping their admiration. A burst of spontaneous applause for that beautiful, courageous, earnest, talented girl—Starla Scruggs, deaf majorette, who stood there in stark relief like a figure out of Greek drama, her face a mask of stylized, implacable emotion, all those mothers a chorus that chanted dismay and bathos through their hands. As Starla bowed and blew kisses from her fingertips, the applause died down until only my mother was clapping—*pop-pop-pop*—telegraphing a message of bewilderment.

"The one thing we're brilliant at is killing off plants," my wife says.

"And breaking wineglasses," I say.

On this Saturday afternoon in April, we're standing in the kitchen of our apartment in Brooklyn, frowning over the withered clematis she'd potted last week. She twiddles the stove's dials, puts the teakettle on a back burner. I'm holding a legal pad scribbled with a list of confirmed yeas for the twins' first birthday party, pen tucked behind my ear. The weather outside is middling, typical of this time of year, that lag between the narcissi and the lilacs. No rain yet but clouds humped and moving like a school of dolphins, gusts swaying the elms along the avenue, buds clinging delicately to the branches, lime green parasols. The pollen count is high.

"Ah—ah—ah—*choooo*," Ellen says theatrically, jiggling her ponytail, hamming it up for the twins in their high chairs. They giggle.

"I watered it every day," I say. "And it got enough light."

"Oy gevalt—just an amazing talent for killing them, even the African violets," she says, pulling down a mug from the cabinet. "We can't even claim the Kevorkian defense." The kettle whistles. She pours, dunks a tea bag, its tag sticking to the rim, English Breakfast. "Heaven help the ficus who ends up here," she says. "Requiescat in pace."

Robyn, Owen's preternaturally serene nurse, ventures into the kitchen, tall and lithe, her strawberry blond hair done up in a French braid. She smiles and nods, bodhisattva-like, slips a lean arm into the refrigerator for a syringe of purple-pink medication, a color almost neon, then withdraws down the hall to his room. For the past hour she's been massaging the ligaments in his hands as he sat floppily in a chair molded for his limp body, reading Dr. Seuss to him, his face alert, his three-year-old mind absorbing the wordplay.

"You're saying we're serial killers?" I ask.

"Maybe not Charles Manson and Susan Atkins," she says, "but from the plants' point of view . . ."

She sets the mug in the sink, leaking tea, peeks into the fridge. "We need applesauce for the babies."

"Plants don't feel pain," I say. "Not like a dog or a cat."

"How do you know there's no such thing as plant pain?"

For the rest of the afternoon we fret over the guest list—*Do you think my boss will really show up? Charles and Konstantin are bringing a red velvet cake, I kid you not*—but an unease roots deep in my mind. From window to window, the light shifts gray to blue, shifts again. At one point I duck into Owen's room, where Robyn is narrating the antics of Thing One and Thing Two. Early on he lost his vowels, his rudimentary consonants, *g* and *d* and *k,* but he seems to be learning something, even in silence. The elms outside cast frilled shadows onto his walls when the sun breaks through to the west, over Sunset Park.

And still it gnaws at me, the agony of the plants.

We attend to the evening's business. Robyn and I do Owen's respiratory treatment in stages: nebulizer, chest physical therapy, the cough assist machine. She suctions sputum from his lungs, readies him for bed. He drifts off before she heads into the bathroom to change out of her scrubs. I spy her next by the front door, dressed in a blouse and wool skirt and heeled boots, waving as she lets herself out. She's meeting someone at a restaurant on Smith Street. Ellen has tended to the twins: a jar of pulped sweet potatoes, some grapes, then clean diapers and a move to their crib. She hums Taps: *Day is done, gone the sun . . .* Already they're tangled in sleep.

All is well, safely rest, God is nigh.

The plants suffer mutely, crabgrass mutilated by lawn mowers, corn skewered for the dinner table, kelp strangling on their own bodies in the tides off Coney Island. I feel their anguish in the apartment's parquet floor, the grain of the wood in Owen's bed, each swirl of bird's-eye maple a severed organ. The cruelty of restaurants, asparagus boiled and plated, arugula lashed and served as a salad course. My mother's irises, writhing in the cups of their languid petals, her roses bared to the knife, flailing their thorns in self-defense.

On Christmas Eve, Starla sits with her family in the pew our family once occupied, flanked by her blond children and her lanky husband, handsome, with salt-and-pepper hair, a cleft chin. Tonight the weather's inclement, the stained-glass windows japanned with sleet, but here inside the sanctuary, the chandelier winks a warm glow. The handbell choir takes its place in the loft, beneath the baptistery, chimes a carillon of "Away in a Manger." There's a raft of poinsettias along the marble-topped Lord's Supper table, in florist poses around the pulpit, a swath of crimson that aches the eyes, beautifully static, petals crisp as wax paper.

Starla's aura still flickers beneath the pounds she's put on, her padded neck. Occasionally an older woman will stare at her from across the sanctuary, remembering a John Philip Sousa march, a baton routine. She'll lean up toward her adult son, her hand gnarled along the cuff of his tweed coat, whisper in his ear a phrase or two that brings it all back.

Beneath Starla the pew's mahogany creaks. The congregants bend forward in their seats, enthralled by the pastor's words. She watches his lips as he preaches a sermon she can't hear.

8

FALL CREEK FALLS

Like a Baptist Cassandra—nerves fraught, voice gravelly—my mother proclaimed that the end of the world was nigh.

Aged thirteen, I was sitting in the passenger seat in our butter-colored Pontiac, parked outside the Red Food store on Ring-gold Road. It was twilight. I was still sweaty and cleated from soccer practice. My mother had just strapped herself behind the steering wheel, her hair teased to a halo of Streisand-like curls. She'd flipped on the radio for the six o'clock news. A skinny, pimpled bag boy ferried paper sacks onto the rear floorboard. A violet light played across the dashboard, easing in a somber, contemplative mood.

The news did not seem dire. *Egypt's leader, Anwar Sadat, has agreed to travel to Jerusalem to address the Knesset,* the newscaster intoned, *an overture to Israel that could lead to a normalization of diplomatic relations.*

My mother rapped her fist on the wheel. "Don't you see, Sugar," she said, her eyes wild. "He's the Antichrist! Just as the Bible prophesied!"

"Who?" I asked, feeling a wave of dread coming off her.

"Sadat!" Her voice was a hushed scream. "What does

Revelation say about the Antichrist? That he will be a so-called peacemaker? All of the other signs have been fulfilled."

I tapped the heels of my cleats together, discomfited less by her vision of the end-time and more by the mania in her voice. As far as I was concerned, the world might end tomorrow, or it might not. The back door slammed shut as she twisted the key in the ignition. We coasted backward and then lurched into drive, buoyed by the torque of her reverie.

"I bet you if you lifted the lock of his hair you'd find '666' etched into his forehead."

"But Mom, I've seen Sadat on television—he's bald."

She was always searching for omens: a comet painting its acetylene fire across a night sky, armies of Huns camped on the lawn, a plane nose-diving into the Sequoyah cooling tower, up on Lake Chickamauga. She couldn't turn her back on us for a minute.

Just a few years earlier, three men with criminal records had hijacked a Southern Airlines DC-9 on a routine flight over Alabama. They'd demanded a ransom of $10 million plus free passage to Havana in exchange for the crew and thirty-one passengers. If their demands weren't met, they'd threatened to crash the plane into the Oak Ridge nuclear plant, igniting a pyroclastic flow to level the Cumberland Plateau, scorching forests of loblolly pine. For almost three days the plane had crisscrossed the country, the hijackers' moves breathlessly narrated by newscasters. At one point they landed at the Chattanooga airport, refueling near a phalanx of police cars parked on the tarmac. An FBI agent, stripped down to a T-shirt and boxer shorts, loped up to the plane and delivered a suitcase containing $2 million, the only amount the hijackers would receive before later surrendering in Havana and releasing their captives, unharmed.

My father had left work early that afternoon, driven straight home to watch the airport drama on our Magnavox set in the basement, my mother's hand idling on his shoulder, a protective gesture, her charm bracelet dangling against his collar. As we watched the plane taxi on the flickering screen, she'd knelt beside me. "Quick, the backyard," she said. "You may see it."

We lived a mile away from the airport, our neighborhood in direct alignment with the runway. I darted outside, into a pocket of silence. There was no one around. A dry season had blanched the grass. The block looked like itself—same crescent of split-level houses, yards glum with weeds and rusty swing sets, telephone poles listing like Towers of Pisa—but a fear colored the moment. I heard a whine overhead, the scream of thrusters, as the plane banked a few hundred feet above, metallic in the clear sky, a yellow smiley face painted on the fuselage like a mark of the Beast.

In 1977, then, the world was crashing around my parents: hijackings, terrorist plots, witchcraft in high schools, bras torched by bands of harpies called "feminists." A society taxed by threats at home and an erosion of trust in its elected leaders. A surge of talk about the "End-time," pastors thundering about the imminent Rapture from their pulpits, books, and television shows and films opining on the tribulations at hand, geared to the faithful who swarmed into churches in advance of the approaching apocalypse.

Like their fellow Baptists, they prayed and prepared. They

attended study groups in the sanctuary. They dutifully read and reread Revelation, attempting to discern its opaque prophesies. *The establishment of Israel?* Check. *The European Common Market?* Check. *And the bit about Babylon? Clearly a reference to the Soviet Union.* The only unfulfilled sign, as my mother scribbled in the margin of her Bible, was the rebuilding of the Jewish Temple in Jerusalem. The Bible's satin ribbon would flutter across the pew's plush cushion as she made notes.

The faithful knew what to do. They devised rituals to keep their kids away from pool halls and pinball arcades. Brother Odie, the youth minister, furnished a dank room beneath the church gymnasium, fitting it out with donated couches, fabric ripped and leaking foam rubber, a beanbag chair, and a vintage highboy table. A Coke machine stood along one wall. As a seventh grader, I was allowed free use of the Youth Lounge. My friends and I would fidget on one of the couches while Renee Sanders, a junior, would pick a guitar, fretting the chords of "I Wish We'd All Been Ready," the theme song from the classic Rapture film, *A Thief in the Night,* which I'd seen five years before:

> *Life was filled with guns and war,*
> *and everyone got trampled on the floor,*
> *I wish we'd all been ready . . .*

This song gave a creepy thrill at the end. We'd all croon the final chorus until, on cue, we'd break off in midsyllable:

> *You've been left behind*
> *You've been left behind*
> *You've been left be——*

We'd stare bug-eyed around the silent room, lost in the fantasy, as Renee would slowly lower the guitar into its case.

⟋⟍⟋◦

The rituals were many, but few offered pleasure. The one notable exception was the annual summer Retreat, when the youth group, grades seven through twelve, laden with knapsacks and sleeping bags, headed out of town en masse to a campground a couple of hours away.

One muggy August afternoon we loaded onto the Greyhound, sang rounds of "Bingo" and "Up with People" as Brother Odie drove us north, around the curves of Signal Mountain and onto the Cumberland Plateau and eventually into Fall Creek Falls State Park. The church had rented the park's recreation center for the week. The twin buildings stood miles from the split-rail gate, secluded in a forest of white oaks and conifers. We filed off the bus and into the dormitory, boys on the ground floor, girls on the upper floor, each claiming a metal bunk with a dingy pallet. Seventh-grade boys occupied the lowest rung on the social ladder, so my friends and I were banished to a windowless alcove, farthest from the bathroom. The four of us pulled our bunks together and curtained them off with Mitch Fulghum's *Happiness is a warm puppy* blanket, Snoopy and Lucy locked in an awkward embrace.

Retreat followed the same daily pattern: after a breakfast of French toast in the rec center's main room, we'd gather with our Bibles and Bic pens while Brother Odie droned on about some passage from Ephesians or Galatians. We'd mumble the obligatory answers to his questions—*nothing but the grace of God, not my will but His be done*—but our thoughts were careening in anticipation of the afternoon: water balloon fights; arts and crafts class; a ten-minute bus ride to the park's spring-fed swimming pool, where Tad Swope would cannonball his six-foot-two frame off the high dive, spraying Barb Draper and Nikki Carson (known as Boom Boom Barb and Foxy Nikki to the pimpled set) as they primped on the pool's edge, ravishing in their string bikinis.

Retreat was celebrated for another, titillating reason: for a whole week we were free. Our parents were fifty miles away, down a mountain's crooked highway, stewing in the valley's soupy air, their preoccupation with a dystopian future. We could sneak off to indulge in some rebellious behavior. Beau Clayton had smuggled a stash of nickel bags in the flannel lining of his sleeping bag; after lights-out he'd hole up in a bathroom stall, rolling joints. Denny Ledford had brought his eight-track player and vinyl case with the complete oeuvres of Led Zeppelin and Lynyrd Skynyrd. A couple of eighth graders once kicked a soccer ball into an upper window, shattering it over one of the hapless Sanders girls and necessitating a tearful trip to the Pikeville clinic for stitches.

There were hints of darker, more enticing transgressions. The minister of music's daughter, sinewy as a ballerina, taught us the Hustle. Cherie Fiske, the youth group's bad girl, would get into trouble for showing up to breakfast in a halter top. Each evening at least one couple, usually Cherie and her latest conquest, would traipse from the woods, clothes disheveled. From the older guys you'd hear rumors: a sixer of Pabst hidden beneath the rec center's cinder blocks, a fifth of Jack Daniel's stowed in someone's footlocker. You'd be inclined to dismiss the rumors until you noticed the guys at Bible Study the next morning, red-eyed, dozing off.

I wasn't sure what I thought about all these teenage libidos in close quarters. I wasn't feeling their frenzy . . . yet. But I *was* bored with the same old, same old, as the lessons from that August—the Fall of Man, *the wages of sin is death*—flitted through my mind like a mountain vapor. Each evening after a dinner of baked chicken and potato salad, we'd sit cross-legged in the courtyard, grouped around the barbecue pit. We'd sing "Pass It On," marshmallows browning on wire coat hangers:

> *You share His love with everyone*
> *You want to pass it on . . .*

The last afternoon we hiked to see Fall Creek Falls, one of the highest waterfalls in the eastern United States. The path tracked down into a gorge fleeced with kudzu and the whisper of rushing water. Single file we descended beneath outcroppings of sandstone, fiddlehead ferns. One of the pious sophomore girls mentioned how God must have gently tapped His finger here, creating this beautiful place.

Close to the falls, the path grew boggy, stones slicked with mist. We clambered toward a jet of water, over two hundred feet high, sluiced into shadows, dousing our Adidas shirts and Top-siders. The path horseshoed behind the falls. A couple of senior boys led us forward. Shivering, we yelled to each other over the roar but couldn't quite communicate.

What we had, though, was unspoken: a richer bond, exponentially greater than the sum of our parts, a ragtag line of teenagers in damp T-shirts and cutoff shorts, shaggy sideburns and Charlie's Angels haircuts. Arms around each other, we peered heavenward through a crystalline veil and wondered what it was all about.

$$\smile\!\!\!\!\!\sim$$

Now, thirty years later, my wife, the vegetarian liberal Jew from California, is curious. "I've Netflixed *Jesus Camp* for the weekend," she tells me on her afternoon check-in call from work. "I want to know more about your tribe."

Whoa. In all our years together—the childless idyll spent in bars in the East Village, sipping vodka gimlets; the tortured odyssey of Owen's first year; the birth of the twins, columns in the foundation of our mature married life—she's never expressed an interest in the Baptists. But children—the sheer fact you've passed along your DNA to these beguiling creatures—can tickle awake those latent tribal cells. Their kicks and smells and babble can catapult you toward traditions you'd sworn to bury years ago.

"Like, what about my tribe?"

"Like, are they as meshugana as the rest of the country thinks?"

"Do you really think you'll find out from a documentary?" I say.

"Well . . . ," she says.

On Saturday afternoon, as a chilly rain drizzles the skeletal elms outside our apartment building in Brooklyn, she slips the DVD into the player and we cuddle our twins. A beanbag chair cradles Owen, our five-year-old, his hips and legs buttressed by pillows. *Jesus Camp* tells the story of a woman evangelical and the camp she runs in North Dakota, called Kids on Fire, where she trains a new generation of Scripture-quoting warriors determined to take back America for Christians. Some of the details strike a chord: the bus ride to a rustic setting, the good-natured joshing, adults hovering over the young flock, the desultory call-and-response of daily Bible study. But some of the scenes jump out at me as extreme: the speaking in tongues, a life-size cutout of George W. Bush, a prayer service centered on abortion. The leaching away of joy.

The credits roll. My wife presses the remote and glares at me, eyebrows arched, an accusation.

"Um, well, it really wasn't like that . . . ," I stammer, my voice betraying a sudden defensiveness.

Or had it been like that?

In fact, my congregation had specifically rejected the notion of speaking in tongues. I'd gotten so much more out of it than a resentment of people who think differently than I do, who might pray to another god. I'd gotten so much more than a peculiar desire to scare children into denouncing even other Protestant faiths as inauthentic.

But what, exactly, *had* I gotten out of it?

Owen relies on various machines to monitor his breathing, the milk that drips, ounce by ounce, through a slit in the wall of his body; but there are no devices to scratch out my own internal fluctuations, no pacemaker for the soul. Over the years I've gravitated toward a different kind of camp, the sugar rush of the city boosting my spirits the way the pulsing ribbon of Fall Creek Falls elevated them years ago. In a near-ecstatic state, I've given myself over to a Picasso retrospective at the Metropolitan Museum; an Annie Proulx or Jhumpa Lahiri story in

The New Yorker; Ellen's Saturday brunches, ciabatta sliced and dipped in egg yolk and baked in the oven, served with French butter and raspberries from the farmers' market at Grand Army Plaza. Ardent husband-and-wife debates on a gamut of topics: ornery doctors, brands of baby food, Park Slope restaurants, Franzen or Díaz? Ten minutes of transcendence, spliced sporadically into each week, each month, each year. A faith in these things, however provisional.

But it's not a clean trade-off. Brooklyn now does not equal Fall Creek Falls then.

Ellen lifts one of the twins from her lap, stands and follows him as he toddles into the kitchen. A moment later I hear her at the counter, humming a Jam song as she dices garlic for our dinner pasta.

I suck in a deep breath. All this endless talk about the End-time was the familiar background music of my adolescence, a jarring if faint melody that played in my head as I learned to serve a volleyball, to glide a razor across a stubbled chin, on those Retreats. Most of all, I'd discovered a sense of spiritual uplift, of oneness with others, by chance on a hike through a gorge, mist on the cheeks, a rainbow shimmering in the humid Tennessee air.

I'm now the same age that my mother was that year Sadat flew to Jerusalem, when she stood rigid and frowning in the church parking lot as I stepped sunburnt and weary from the bus, home from Fall Creek Falls, literally a happy camper. I obsess, as she did, about my children's safety, though without her religious certitude. And in many ways, the song's the same: political scandals, the drumbeat of war, a chronic dread itching beneath the skin.

But here's the part I don't tell my wife: I still feel that old foreboding. It surfaces in nightmares, the images serrated, sinister. An empty, menacing subway platform at night. A gang of thugs pursuing me through a charred, abandoned city. The whine of hijacked planes as they slam into sleek skyscrapers, a stream of flame and ash falling, falling toward me.

9

THE BOOK OF LAMENTATIONS

That summer, suddenly, sex: the scoop-necked T-shirts all three Sanders girls wore to Sunday School, brazenly exposing the bronzed northern regions of their chests; the dick jokes the senior boys traded during Youth Choir rehearsal; those field trips to the swimming cove near Chickamauga Dam, where the teenagers from the Children's Home would defy the rules and stroke out to the buoys so they could hang on to the cables and feel each other up beneath the waterline, out of view of the chaperones. With school out, the entire youth group, grades seven through twelve, unfolded their bodies like tropical flowers famished for sunlight, all scents and petals, stamens and pistils.

All kinds of things were going on. An uptick in four-letter words, muttered under the breath or lustily shouted when out of parental range. Suggestive things: in the crawl space beneath the church gym; behind the closed door of the Youth Lounge, notorious for its hippie aura, its throw rugs and lava lamps. Kyle Allison and Karen Sanders with their arms draped around each other. Denny Ledford and Tad Swope out in the parking lot, an eight-track player propped on the hood of a Trans Am, staging their own discotheque and egging on the girls to thrust their hips: *Do a little dance, make a little love, get down tonight.*

All around us wafted the perfume of forbidden fruit, cracked open and oozing its juices.

I, too, was distracted. Fourteen years old, I'd spend each hour-long worship service focused on my own inspirational project, tuning out Brother Virgil's sermons to read all sixty-six books of the Bible in order, from Genesis to Revelation. In two years I'd pushed through a brisk narrative headwind—the Pentateuch and the histories, all those meticulous laws and corrupt kings—easing up a bit with the sumptuous Psalms and cryptic Ecclesiastes. Then back in the winter I'd tumbled into the Song of Solomon, that wise ruler's sensuous paean to romantic love. I'd felt light-headed and filthy after I finished its charged chapters.

7:2 Thy navel is like a round goblet, which wanteth not liquor: thy belly is like an heap of wheat set about with lilies.

7:3 Thy two breasts are like two young roes that are twins.

7:4 Thy neck is as a tower of ivory; thine eyes like the fishpools in Heshbon, by the gate of Bath-rabbim: thy nose is as the tower of Lebanon which looketh toward Damascus.

Now, though, I'd begun to regard all those hours devoted to the Scriptures as a child's hobby outgrown, like soapbox derby or gluing a model battleship from a kit. In the arid wilderness of the Prophets, I'd stalled out, bored witless by Jeremiah, with the next book, the slim, eponymous Lamentations, unlikely to reignite my ardor. I longed to flip back to the Song of Solomon, that tingle below the belt.

One evening, in the languid hour between dinner and family devotional, my parents tried to talk to me. They nudged my bedroom door ajar while I was reading the Bible at my desk. My mother loitered in the hall as my father scuffled in, pausing next to the closet door. He avoided eye contact, his face puffy and florid, like a priest's. He blurted out his spiel in fragments—*birds and the bees, when a woman gives herself to her husband, such a precious treasure from God.* His train of thought seemed to derail at the missionary position in a pitch-black room, all gritted teeth and clumsy contortions. I suspected my mother had put him up to it.

"You understand?" he concluded, finally looking at me, eyes blue and rheumy, saggy at the corners.

I nodded, eager to smother the shared misery of this moment. My mother elbowed past him then, exultant, as though both of us had answered a question correctly on *The $20,000 Pyramid,* an instant before the timer's horn. I imagined her rapturous in a spotlight, an updraft of balloons and ticker tape. "Let me tell you something, Sugar," she said, twitchy with adrenaline. "The act of love is a gift unique to a husband and wife, sent special delivery from the Lord!"

Her voice boomed like a game show host's. "There may be girlfriends along the way—not for a *while,* till you get your driver's license—but they'll all fade away when you meet that someone, the way your daddy forgot all about that German woman when he met me. Maybe next year, if you got your eye on someone, you can ask her to church."

A salty taste at the back of my throat, an oyster of mucus. "Ru—Ruth," I said. "You knew about her."

Although a large man, my father seemed to shrink behind her, cowering in the blaze of her enthusiasm. If he'd hoped to do this his way, he'd failed completely. She was taking over, as usual. "Of course I know all about her," she said. "She was just the warm-up act for me!" She did a couple of jitterbug steps, patted herself on the chest.

"It was a tad more serious than that," he said, glancing away, voice gruff. "Engaged briefly, after all."

"She worked at the PX on your base," my mother said, grinning, bowing to a partner somewhere in the vicinity of my dresser. "Hardly serious."

"Why did you lie to me about Ruth?" I said.

"I've had enough," my father said, turning his back on the folly he'd unleashed. My mother halted her impromptu dance, glared at me, her lips hard. She hated it when I called her on falsehoods she'd uttered. She hated it more when I stumbled onto something that defied a convenient, straight-out-of-the-Good-Book explanation. Like sex, slippery with half-truths and innuendos, sparking loopy behavior from otherwise rational people.

"I have absolutely no idea what you're talking about," she said, pivoting on her heels to leave me alone with Jeremiah, his *woe untos*, his *thus saith the Lords*. Only after she'd closed the door again did I realize neither of them had actually spoken the word *sex* itself.

Something had shifted. I felt like a beachcomber working a remote sweep of dunes. A tide of testosterone had hauled in a flotsam strange to me, ugly as plastic jugs and rusted cans, stinking of shit. All the transcendent moments I'd known—

my baptism, Glorieta, Fall Creek Falls—now tasted cloyingly sweet in my mouth, like day-old butter mints served at a wedding reception. I wanted to spit them out.

Deep down I'd already confessed the truth to myself: I was addled by that electricity, girls in halter tops and boys with smoldering looks. I *loved* using words like *shit* and *damn* when hanging out with the youth group on the gym steps on Wednesday evenings, in the hiatus between early supper in the Fellowship Hall and the midweek worship service.

Once a sophomore bully, Sonny Robeson, called me a queerbait just like Jimmy Norway, the elfin bachelor who sang in the choir and could hit all the soprano notes *fortissimo* in the "Hallelujah Chorus." I was dimly aware of what the term meant—an invisible cordon drawn around Jimmy, lumping him with the others that the congregation had silently segregated but refused to excommunicate. Patricia Thatcher, the brawny women's softball coach who drove a motorcycle and insisted that everyone call her Pat. Brad Alverson, who embroidered during worship service, turning out monogrammed sheets and duvet covers prized by my mother and her friends. Jimmy, Pat, Brad: discreetly shunted into niches they might not have chosen for themselves. Misfits all, both cherished and repudiated, hidden away in plain sight.

I flipped Sonny off, and he threw a punch. When my parents asked about the bruise, I said I'd tripped on the basketball court. It seemed so easy to lie these days.

But a backlash was coming. I could sense something afoot among the church elders and their wives, brows puckered.

Like the Hebrews in the Old Testament, they found a scapegoat. In the minutes before each service, as Miss Eula, the prim organist, played an overture and people gathered in the sanctuary, there were whispered conversations, hands cupped around lips and ears. From where I sat with my parents and sister—left side, two pews from the front, downwind from the pulpit—I'd hear a chorus from decorous social pillars such as Mrs. Welch and Mrs. Sanders, their voices indignant and judgmental, echoing along the ceiling's vault, buzzing like Furies.

"Is Cherie Fiske out of her cotton-picking mind? Braless in church? Someone should say something to her mother."

"Dee Fiske? That poor woman don't have enough sense to get in out of the rain. Divorced, you know."

"My Mandy told me Cherie wore hot pants when the youth went to the roller rink, and that she couple-skated with Martin Draper and he kept his hand in her butt pocket the whole time."

"I heard she wore a skimpy bikini at the dam and swam out to the buoys to smooch with Denny Ledford."

"My Mitch said he went looking for a basketball in the gym closet and caught Cherie and Martin in a lip-lock."

"My Renee said she saw Cherie and Denny on the couch in the Youth Lounge, curled up beneath an afghan blanket, *supposedly* reading a book, and when she stood up her pants were unzipped."

"Martin Draper and Denny Ledford! My land, that girl's playing those boys off one another."

Two grades ahead of me, Cherie Fiske had been stigmatized for years: the daughter of a single, down-on-her-luck mother rumored to espouse women's lib; a girl gawky and airheaded, with Coke-bottle glasses and zit cream splotching her rubbery face, a smile that kinked up at the corners, like a cat's. The long slog through puberty had kept Cherie in a cocoon of isolation, but just a few months ago she'd abruptly emerged with contact lenses, clear, lucent skin, and thirty pounds converted into an hourglass figure. With a vengeance she made up for all that time lost in the adolescent gulag, soaking up the attention of the older boys in youth group. She'd saunter into the Fellowship Hall, carrot orange hair viscous with Alberto VO5, blouse tied to reveal a midriff and fulsome hips. Even a couple of the deacons ogled her. I secretly enjoyed watching her cavort in her new leggy, jiggly self, but I wasn't going to say anything to my parents, risk summoning their ire.

The Drapers had dropped into a nervous, defensive crouch. Mr. Draper was a lawyer and chairman of the deacons; Mrs. Draper had just been named director of the Women's Missionary Union, or WMU. With one daughter off at college, they lived with their teenagers in a French provincial in Riverview and were among my parents' closest friends, at the center of the network of families that dominated the congregation's affairs, yet the two of them seemed a fragile levee against the pounding tide of Cherie Fiske's sexual awakening. Martin Draper, their son, was a junior at the country day school, an A student whose paintings had just won a national contest. Swarthy, brooding, creative, next year's front runner for Youth Week Pastor and destined for a ream of college scholarships, Martin cultivated a dual mystique of golden boy and rebel artist, aloof, not of this world.

Each worship service Martin would stare goggle-eyed at Cherie's cleavage, a hymnal opened facedown in his lap. In the nubile fullness of Cherie's breasts, the Drapers glimpsed the horrific specter of Martin's undoing, and hence their own.

One Sunday after church, my mother and I ran into Mrs. Draper in the parking lot, and the topic of Cherie surfaced immediately. Dazed by the heat, I shuffled from foot to foot, suit sticking to my skin. Mrs. Draper said she'd considered raising her concerns with Cherie's mother, woman to woman, but couldn't quite figure out the icebreaker to that conversation. She said she felt sorry for Dee Fiske, how she struggled. As she pointed out to my mother, it wasn't like the Drapers were against single women—just look how much her husband had done for his secretary, newly divorced Lorelei Carson, whose daughter, Nikki, was thirteen, the same age as Barb Draper and my sister. For weeks he'd driven Lorelei home to her modest bungalow on the city's east side, had stayed for dinner and a little Bible study, and had personally led her to the Lord. Brother Virgil had baptized Lorelei and Nikki Carson in a special mother-daughter ceremony.

"How inspiring," my mother said. "That's a godly man you have there."

"I appreciate that," Mrs. Draper said. "Can't tell you how much."

My mother brought up the possibility of Denny Ledford as a counterweight. "Cherie seems quite infatuated with him," she noted. A moonfaced senior, Denny was the son of Brother Von Ledford, the lead tenor in the adult choir and famous for his operatic solos and leonine mane of hair. Something of an embarrassment to his father, Denny was always getting into scrapes, wrecking his car or skipping algebra to smoke reefer; the antithesis of Martin. More in Cherie's league, according to my mother.

"I bet you a cup of coffee she'll end up with Denny," my

mother said, clasping her friend's gloved hand. "Birds of a feather."

⌒‿⌒

No wonder I'd bogged down on the cusp of Lamentations: I was keen to swap religious passion for the more earthly kind. Back in the winter, I'd gone with a school friend to a lock-in at the Methodist church across Brainerd Road, where I'd met my own siren, Ashley Wheeler, a seventh grader at the girls' school and frequently described as "physically mature," more womanly in the Barb Draper or Nikki Carson mode than other thirteen-year-olds, unlike my flat-as-a-board sister or the brainy, pixieish Mandy Welch.

In some respects Ashley seemed a ladylike version of Cherie Fiske, pinning back her strawberry blond hair with grosgrain headbands and sporting Fair Isle yoke sweaters and flannel pants, Lilly Pulitzer sundresses and Pappagallo flats in warmer seasons. But the girl was captive to drives of her own, as I'd discovered during a spirited game of Truth or Dare in a darkened broom closet off the Methodist Fellowship Hall. We'd groped each other while her friends stood guard outside, tussling against mops and pails, my boner jammed against her crotch until it chafed. We'd finally pulled apart when we heard a rap on the closet door, a code alerting us to the nearby presence of a chaperone. We'd straightened our clothes, opened the door. In the chiaroscuro light, Ashley stared at me as though she'd had the wind knocked out of her, wiped a trace of my saliva from her neck, and pronounced, "Aunt Berta was right: once you try Baptist, you'll *never* go back!"

In the months since we'd talked on the phone, gone to a

couple of Afterglows, post-Sunday-evening-service socials for the youth group, hosted at a residence or lake house. The Afterglows were our parents' opening salvo: apple cider and s'mores and a little television, mandatory clean fun. My father chauffeured Ashley and me in the Pontiac so our moves were always monitored. Once, at the Welchs' farm, out past Lake Chickamauga, she and I had snuck off to the barn for tonguing and a feel, but the relationship still seemed overly chaste to me, poorly defined.

Boyfriend-girlfriend? Going together? I couldn't stand it. Rather than fade, the memory of the Methodist lock-in had morphed into a nightly pornographic cartoon, Cubist penises and vulvas, breasts canted onto shoulders and arms, pubic hair wild as a sea anemone, rough as sandpaper. If I could just place the two of us in a different context, away from baleful parental eyes . . .

Brother Odie, the youth minister, was planning a day trip to Six Flags Over Georgia, near Atlanta. Maybe that would do it. But I had to finagle this just right; otherwise my parents would suspect that I wasn't the saint they thought they'd reared, that I wasn't immune to the hormones breaking like surf over the youth group.

One night just before bed, as we wrapped up family devotional in our living room, I asked my parents—tentatively, respectfully—if I could ask Ashley. My father was sitting in his faux Louis Quatorze chair, tie loose and sparse hair combed over, socked feet atop scuffed loafers. Already in her Snoopy nightgown, my sister, thirteen years old but still a little girl in many ways, had crawled into his lap and was dozing against his shoulder. He yawned and glanced at my mother. She'd put her July issue of *Baptist & Reflector* on the coffee table and was swigging a mug of Sanka.

She rolled her eyes. "Sugar, you been talking to that girl an awful lot. It's not like you're dating."

"Please," I begged.

"You're too *young* to *date,*" she said, her words pricked with annoyance and some deeper, hurtful emotion, punching her mug hand for emphasis and raining decaf on the carpet. "Gosh durn it."

"Serves you right, Cholly," my father said. "Acting like a banshee."

Since my mother's emergency surgery last year, a rushed hysterectomy, they'd seemed wary around each other, bickering constantly. *Are you gonna get off your duff and fix that dishwasher? All you do these days is nag, nag, nag.* That afternoon they'd fought over late bills, the electricity cut off for a few hours. My mother had driven away in the Pontiac to calm her nerves.

"Well, bullpoopy on *you,*" she said now, sticking out her tongue.

"You can ask Ashley if you want," my father said. "If Bud Wheeler says it's okay, it's okay."

"Don't like where this is going—" my mother said.

"Just watch it," my father interrupted.

I kissed them each good night on the cheek and scurried downstairs to my room to place the call, shutting the door behind me. I kept the telephone, a fourteenth birthday present, in its cradle on the floor next to the bed, cord lassoed around my boxed Lord of the Rings. After slipping off my shorts and tank top, I reached for the phone, hesitated. I didn't even know Ashley's favorite color, her favorite flower. Green or yellow? Rose or camellia?

What a loser. I needed some expert advice, a simpatico friend to bolster my courage, so I dialed the Allisons' number. Mrs.

Allison answered with a chirpy greeting. "Let's see, Kyle's gone off with his daddy and the deacons to visit the shut-ins, so that must mean it's Craig downstairs in the basement." I could hear a stereo playing up-tempo lounge music, the kind my parents had danced to when we'd celebrated their anniversary at the Loret Club, Al Martino or Perry Como. *When you find your own true love you will know it—by her smile, by the look in her eyes.* "Fogey music," my sister had called it, twirling a tiny paper umbrella in her virgin mai tai as our parents did a fox-trot, frowning, across the Formica floor. Married twenty-five years, frayed along the edges.

"Not sure what he's up to, but let me call him," Mrs. Allison said.

After a series of shouted *Craig, phone!*s, my friend picked up, breathing heavy. "Great timing," he said. "Typical."

"What's the matter?"

"I was looking at Kyle's magazines." Craig's older brother had stashed away some *Playboy*s and *Penthouse*s behind a panel of Sheetrock in their dad's welding workshop. "Redheads with bazooms the size of watermelons. Shit."

"My parents said I could ask Ashley Wheeler to Six Flags."

"Oh yeah, that Methodist girl," Craig said. A pause, a current of titillation. "Damn, you got into that chick's pants yet?"

"Oh yeah, sure," I lied.

"Right on," he said. "You finger her?"

I couldn't quite picture the anatomical transaction, but I'd die before I'd admit it. "Sure, sure," I said.

"No shit," he said. "Smelled like fish, right? Stinky pinkie?"

A barrage of images, pungent odors: my mother's fish sticks, batter-coated and deep-fried in the cooker; my father grilling salmon steaks on the patio; the main course at church supper in the Fellowship Hall, catfish fillets breaded and dressed with lemon slices and laid out on banquet tables.

"Shit, yeah," I said. "Reeeeally fishy."

I heard him swallow, a staccato of breath. "Only seen her at the Afterglows," he said. "Those look like some humongous bazooms. Damn shit."

"Oh yeah," I said. "She's big. Damn shit."

"Almost as big as Barb or Nikki." It was common knowledge among our youth group that Craig wanted to get it on with one of those curvy thirteen-year-olds. On our recent outing to the swimming cove, when we were all sunning on our towels, he'd literally drooled over Barb's breasts, an embarrassment that quickly circulated from the seniors right down to the seventh graders.

"Bet you love sucking on 'em," Craig said.

"Yeah," I said. "Looooove it."

"You fucker!" he said admiringly.

"Fucker yeah!" I said.

"But you're stuck on third base," he opined. "Don't quite know how to slide into home."

Wasn't Frenching third base?

"Um, yeah," I said. "Exactly."

"Here's what you do," Craig said, settling into his customary advisory role, some voyeuristic urge sated for the moment. "Kyle told me. You could try it at Six Flags, maybe in the Sky Buckets, but maybe better to wait for someplace more private. The goal is to boink her, right, my main man?"

"Sure," I said, feeling a tightening in my groin. "Shit damn."

"First you kiss her romantically, some tongue," he said.

"Then you unbutton her shirt and stick your hand in." He paused again. I sensed a dart of suspicion. "You know how to unhook a bra clasp, right?"

"Shit yeah," I said. "Do it all the time."

"You fucker!" he said brightly, the suspicion erased.

"You fucker!" I said.

The fantasy propelled him along. A girl's pleasure: now *that* was far more intriguing than anything we'd learned in Sunday School or Church Training. "Once you touch her titties, she'll let you do anything," Craig said. "So you kiss her and squeeze gently but keep one eye open so's you can see what you're doing. Then wiggle her shirt off. Then you suck on her nipples till they're hard as bullets."

I could taste metal along my tongue, weirdly erotic.

"With your other hand you unzip her jeans and slide your hand into her panties, down into her bush."

More images: my mother's treasured rhododendrons, the azalea hedge behind the church gym, pruned topiary outside the sanctuary.

"Then you're basically heading for home," Craig said. "Just kiss down from her titties along her stomach and then kiss her poochie."

"Yeah," I whispered hoarsely.

"Girls love it when you kiss and lick their poochie."

". . . ."

"You there?"

"Um . . . yeah," I said.

"Look, I gotta go," he said. "Got to hide those *Playboys* before my dad gets back. See you on the van. Just remember: kiss and lick the poochie. That will get you some coochie-coochie!" He imitated Charo on *The Love Boat,* laughed at his own joke.

"Um, yeah."

"Let me know once you've boinked her and I'll tell Kyle and he'll tell Sonny Robeson so's he won't call you queerbait just like Jimmy Norway no more."

". . . . ."

"It's all about the tongue," he said. "Adiós."

I hung up the phone and sprawled back onto my bed, dizzy and nauseated, like the time I'd bounced furiously on the Twichells' trampoline only to lose my balance and fall. My dick throbbed, poking from the slit in my boxers. What if my dad walked in right now? I snapped the band to cover my bulge. I'd read something about the remedy of cold showers, or maybe Craig had told me, but at this hour I couldn't turn on the spigots without my parents wondering, so I rolled off the bed and sat down at my desk and flipped open the Bible, tossing aside the leather bookmark I'd made last year at Fall Creek Falls.

The Book of Lamentations, blessedly brief after Isaiah and Jeremiah. I could probably read it in one sitting. I glided right through the chapters, my heart still burning its high octane.

> 4:21 Rejoice and be glad, O daughter of Edom, that dwellest in the land of Uz; the cup also shall pass through unto thee: thou shalt be drunken, and shalt make thyself naked.
>
> 4:22 The punishment of thine iniquity is accomplished, O daughter of Zion; he will no more carry thee away into captivity: he will visit thine iniquity, O daughter of Edom; he will discover thy sins . . .
>
> 5:7 Our fathers have sinned, and are not; and we have borne their iniquities.

Absent, sinning fathers, their vices passed along like traits, like left-handedness or brown eyes, marking their children. *That's a godly man you have there.* A daughter, drunken and naked, her sins discovered, those illicit acts of flesh always, always laid bare. *She wore a skimpy bikini at the dam and swam out to the buoys.* Her punishment meted out: the lushness of a body both tart and sweet, like honeysuckle.

I closed the Bible in defeat and sidled back into bed. Beneath the sheet, I peeled down the boxers and circled my thumb and forefinger around the mushroom head, the sensation still foreign to me even though I'd done this a few times.

Lick the poochie. Get some coochie-coochie.

Ashley, I want to toochie your poochie, smoochie your poochie.

Ashley, Ashley.

I stroked the shaft for a moment and then curled onto my belly and humped the mattress until my breath jerked in my throat.

. . . . . .

. . . . . .

I was everywhere and nowhere, hips down in a seep of my own fluid. A pang in my chest: new to me, old as the race. After I pulled my boxers back on, I stripped the sheets from the bed and wadded and threw them into the wicker hamper by the closet door.

Craig had mentioned Six Flags, maybe one of the rides, like the Sky Buckets or the Spindletop. The amusement park offered all sorts of inviting opportunities, like roller coasters. I imagined Ashley clinging to me, squealing, as our car corkscrewed around the track. The log flume, with its tingling splash at the end. The San-Augustine-style haunted castillo; with her fear of vampire-costumed employees, images of ghosts projected onto a dry-ice fog, Ashley would wrap

herself around me, so close I'd smell the peppermint damp-
ness of her skin.

I realized I hadn't called her yet, reached down to the floor
for the receiver. Just like that, without a twinge of guilt or even
reflection, I abandoned my Bible project, right at the book of
Lamentations.

⁓

Since our arrival in the late morning, after a two-hour bus ride,
the youth group had thinned out across Six Flags. My sister and
her clique of seventh graders had opted for a train ride along
the perimeter, complete with a phony armed robbery, masked
bandits boarding through the caboose. Tad Swope racked up
laps on the antique cars, playing his tinny transistor radio: *Hey,
baby baby, I'm your telephone man, just show me where you want
it and I'll put it where I can.* Most of the older guys had rushed
to the Great American Scream Machine, a roller coaster that
clattered and swooped on whitewashed pilings. Craig and my
other good friend, the athletic Trudie Parham, had heeded my
unspoken desire to pair off with Ashley, alone, and had wandered off toward the bumper cars.

Ashley and I had formed a plan: the Dahlonega Mine Train
and log flume and the Spindletop, a detour to the pizza parlor
and maybe a performance at the Chevy Show, one of those
Up With America! extravaganzas left over from the Bicentennial. First stop: the Great Gasp, a parachute ride that shot up
along cables to drop gently to the concrete apron below. As the
attendant strapped us into place, I pinched the small of Ashley's back. She giggled, kicked her feet. We rose two hundred
feet to the top, where the basket swayed for a moment . . . we

surveyed the landscape, spotty groves along the Chattahoochee River and farther off the sawtooth skyline of downtown Atlanta. A breath wrenched in my chest as we plummeted.

"Yee-haawww!" I shouted my best rebel yell.

"Mercy oh my," Ashley screamed, shifting with gravity to brush my shoulder.

After the Great Gasp and a wet slide down the log flume, we snacked on a couple of pepperoni slices, careful not to dribble grease onto our polo shirts or Ashley's madras skirt. We drifted past the castillo and a Victorian carousel, toward the park's back acreage.

"Where're you taking me, devil?" she said, batting her eyes.

"My all-time favorite ride."

Outside the Spindletop's entrance, we bumped into Barb Draper and Nikki Carson with paper cones of sherbert, lips tinted pink and purple. Between mouthfuls they were singing off-key:

Shake your groove thing, shake your groove thing, yeah yeah!
Show 'em how we do it now, show 'em how we do it now!

They shimmied their shoulders in sync, dressed identically in embroidered blouses and khaki shorts and cork sandals, blond hair gel-sculpted. Both girls wore gold add-a-bead necklaces.

"Hey, y'all!" Barb said, flapping her hand.

"We was just going into the Spindletop," Nikki said.

Ashley complimented the matching outfits. "How did y'all manage that one?" she said.

Barb and Nikki exchanged a glance, a hoot of knowing laughter. "Don't you get it," Nikki said. "We're sisters!"

She pronounced the word like *seestoors,* a private joke, more laughter.

"You're that girl from the Methodist church," Barb said.

"I think we should go in," I said.

We made small talk, Ashley shy, buffeted by the girls' boisterous, off-color humor. Nikki combed polished nails through her hair, vamping just in case some cute guy was scoping her from farther back in the line.

"Where's Martin?" I asked Barb.

"Home studying for the SAT, like he even needs to. His college counselor thinks he'll get into Duke and Vanderbilt, maybe Princeton."

"Course he thought *someone else* was coming today," Nikki said, rolling her eyes. "Couldn't bear the thought of seeing that slut, I guess."

"Well, he thought wrong," Barb said, slapping her friend's outstretched hand.

"Gimme five!"

"On the side," Nikki said, slapping back.

"In the *hole.*"

"You got soul!" They collapsed against each other, squinting with mirth, a fit triggered by some connotation of the word *hole.* It dawned on me that they were talking and joking around some explosive, scandalous secret.

"Hey, y'all know why Cherie didn't come today?" I said.

Barb passed through the turnstile and halted on the Spindletop's threshold, feigning a glum face and an accent more drawl than British. "My deah, don't yew know? Lady Cherie Fiske is indisposed today."

"Uh-*huuuhhhhhh!*" Nikki squealed.

Ashley blushed and held back for a moment. I coaxed her into the Spindletop's circular well, fifteen feet deep. A park employee instructed our group of twenty adults and teenagers to press feet and shoulders against the curved foam wall. The motor growled on and the well spun, picking up speed, flattening us. A sensation burned along my groin, more intense than what I'd felt on the Great Gasp. A bulge rose in my shorts. The metal floor dropped, centrifugal force sticking us to the wall. I glanced at Ashley: she'd closed her eyes, hair loose and swathed along her neck like a veil, dewdrops of perspiration on her cheeks and brow. Beyond her, Barb and Nikki shrieked. Barb had turned herself upside down.

"Le Freak, c'est chic, freak out!" she said, high-pitched, as though she'd just breathed in helium.

Gradually the rotation slowed and we all eased dizzily into our own dimension, skidded to the floor, and threaded our way back through the turnstiles. My bulge had deflated. Outside the Spindletop's gate, we clutched the rail for balance.

I wanted to discount Barb's gossip as the cattiness of a girl with a vested interest in the matter. Her brother, after all. But had something serious happened, something that had propelled Cherie toward Denny and away from Martin? Something our parents were determined to quash?

"Too bad Cherie couldn't make it," I said. "She seems to struggle, even with her looks."

"That slut!" Nikki said. "What do you expect from a girl who wears hooker outfits to worship service?"

Ashley ducked her chin, embarrassed by all the Baptist schadenfreude on display.

"I know one thing for sure," Barb said. "Denny Ledford is welcome to her. Sheesh."

"She gives him blow jo——" Nikki blurted out before Barb clapped her hand over her friend's mouth, snickering and spanking her butt. I felt as mortified as Ashley. Some strange choreography was swirling around me and these girls and the Spindletop, beyond the amusement park and the river, disquieting arabesques in the summer glare. Something sinister was happening offstage, out of view, in swimming coves and down on the floorboards of Pontiacs and on the hoods of Camaros; in shadowed crevices like the crawl spaces beneath the floor of the church gym, back in Chattanooga. A dance I couldn't quite see clearly; an opera sung in a minor key, in a language I couldn't discern.

"Chevy Show starts at three. Hear it's got some great sound effects," I said.

Nikki said that she wanted to try the Great American Scream Machine before she had anything else to eat. This gave Ashley and me a clean out. We all shook hands. "See y'all back at the entrance," Barb called from over her shoulder, blowing kisses before she melted into a crowd flowing toward the roller coaster. "Have fun!"

Those words had just spilled out. *Hole. Slut. Blow job.* Raunchy words, even ugly; undeniably arousing. If Ashley was put off in any way, if she'd somehow connected those words to our own wiry, unproven bodies, she didn't let on. I held her hand as we walked silently toward the Chevy Show's blue sphere, puzzling over the gauntlet Barb and Nikki had unwittingly thrown down in front of me.

At the end of August there came a clear Sunday evening with a chill and a tang of pine needles, a whisper of autumn the next day would kill off with ninety-degree temperatures and stifling humidity. I could feel the change in the air. My mother had already driven my sister and me to P & S for our Trapper Keepers, to Loveman's downtown to stockpile chinos and Lacoste sweaters. I hoped to continue my relationship with Ashley past Labor Day and into the school year, hoped for something more tangible, lasting.

For the final Afterglow, the youth were heading out to the Allisons' for milk shakes and Mississippi mud cake. My father had given me special permission to take Ashley, agreeing to drive us so long as we attended the service before and listened to Brother Virgil's sermon. He'd allowed us to sit in the balcony—as he'd said, he trusted us—while he'd join my mother and sister in our family's pew on the lower level. He'd even asked me to hold on to the Pontiac keys.

Aha.

Five minutes into the service, Ashley and I snuck out of the balcony. There were maybe a dozen adults in the pews there, a huddle of teenagers along the rail, Cherie sitting apart from the others and staring straight ahead, her mascara tear-smeared and her hair unruly, with Denny and Martin glowering on opposite sides of the aisle. Craig offered an enthusiastic thumbs-up as we slipped down the stairs. Outside, across Mayfair Avenue, the light had dimmed. My father had parked the Pontiac down by the Dumpster. I fumbled with his key chain. Ashley cocked her glossy pageboy to one side, gave me a coy smile. "Hold on a sec . . . while I . . . insert the . . . *key,*" I said, dragging out the sentence suggestively, but her face remained placid, hard to read.

I unlocked the back door and we climbed in. We slouched down in the vinyl seat and embraced, pressed lips together, and opened mouths, my lower lip nicked by her braces. What had Craig said? Kiss her romantically? She flinched when I applied pressure. I gripped her hand and guided it to the pole in my jeans, but she shrugged me away.

We kissed for a while. She'd closed her eyes, so I gingerly unbuttoned her blouse and traced my fingertips along the cups of her bra to the clasp, a tiny metal spider poised on a gossamer web. I couldn't figure out how to unhook it—no one had ever coached me on what to do, despite my fib to Craig—so I tugged the fabric and ferreted the breast out, the spider barbed against my knuckles.

Ashley, Ashley.

"Ouch, don't," she murmured.

We slid farther down in the seat. With my thumb I teased the nipple, the raised skin around it. Was that an areola? Craig had said something about an areola.

She pushed me away and sat upright, fixed her bra and shirt. "I think we should go back in now," she said.

Had I misread her smiles, the hungry way she'd mashed her mouth to mine?

"You sure?" I said.

"I like you a lot, but I want to go back inside."

We arranged our clothes and got out of the car. I locked it again, my erection flattened in frustration and shame. Ashley primped her bangs, avoiding eye contact. The lot was packed with cars but bereft of people, with the exception of the rent-a-cop in his Jeep parked behind the Dumpster, chin lodged against the steering wheel, mouth open in a snore. We could hear a chatter of mockingbirds along Mayfair Avenue.

Back inside the sanctuary, we crept up to the balcony and

sat down on the first pew, four inches of plush gold cushion between us, then six, then eight. Sermon concluded, Brother Virgil was teeing the invitational hymn, "Would you please turn to 'Just As I Am, Without One Plea.' Christ is waiting for you down here at the front." One of the elders had bumped up the lights, breaking the fever that had plagued me for weeks. Craig looked over at us, smirking with questions I'd hear later on the phone: *What did I tell ya about the tongue, right?* I glanced sidewise at Ashley: she was obsessively smoothing her hair, lips tight. Already she was moving away from me.

Down by the rail, Cherie had wiped off mascara from her cheeks with a Kleenex, uncovering a fresh outbreak of acne. She had locked into an eye argument with Martin, who sat two pews away, his face dark with hurt. I watched them for the hymn's duration, furious accusations and venomous curses conducted in silence. No one came forward that evening, no new professions of faith or transfers of membership from other congregations. No one shambled down the aisle to join our community.

Brother Virgil asked us to stand for the benediction, "Holy, Holy, Holy," its rich major chords evoking a happy throng before the Lord's throne at the end of time, drained of all carnal lusts, the dross of the body washed away.

Holy, holy, holy! Lord God Almighty!
Early in the morning our song shall rise to thee.

Our voices lifted in unison, but as the verses wore on—*All the saints adore thee, casting down their golden crowns around the glassy sea*—I heard a low, thrumming descant, voices building steadily beneath the refrain, an alternate chorus rising and eddying around the gilt chandelier long after Brother Virgil's *amen*. It would echo for months, years.

"That girl's a disgrace—no wonder Dee Fiske hasn't shown her face in weeks."

"Only the Lord knows how Martin Draper has held it together to get his scholarship, after his daddy walked out on the family."

"I hear Barb Draper has had some . . . difficulty with the situation."

"Well, the sins of the father and all that."

"I hear Lorelei Carson had the audacity to wear white at the wedding."

"My Mandy told me Barb and Nikki wore matching bridesmaids' dresses and are now calling themselves step*seestoors,* whatever that means."

"I told my Mitch to just read the Bible cover to cover and do what his parents tell him to, he'll be all right in life."

"I told my Lissy, whenever she feels Satan tempting her, to just talk to the Lord."

"I told my Craig that the road to Heaven is narrow but straight and true."

This chorus hovers there, drawn out like an ellipsis . . . I pass through the procession of Ashleys after Ashley—Megan and Brenda and Katy and Liz—finally docking in the safe harbor of marriage, body thicker now, flecks of gray in my receding hair. But I still can't shake that music, how its syncopation jars even the most grounded of lives, its melody now transposed to a minor, malevolent key, tamping down the joyous harmonies of sex; all the climactic brays and orgasmic squeals collapsed to *betrayal* and *divorce, Bunch of good-for-nothings in that family* and *I heard he married a Jewish girl up in New York*—lyrics heard in dread as they swell outward to cloak the whole earth, a lamentation.

10

GREEN EYES

Craig Allison said:

This is a true story, y'all. I went to elementary school with a girl named Misti Dawn Cantrell and her parents was divorced and she lived with her momma out by the Rolling Hills golf club but her brother lived with their daddy in Suck Creek. He was going with this girl and this happened to this girl's sister. Think her name was Lee Ann.

Lee Ann was a senior at Red Bank: popular, a majorette. Dated this football player named Darrell. They looked great together. She looked kind of like Cheryl Ladd and he looked kind of like Robby Benson. Anyways, the week after graduation, they decided to spend a romantic evening at Chickamauga Battlefield, parking right over there by Wilder Tower—her parents were Church of God of Prophecy and his were strict Baptists, so they had to drive way the hell out in the Georgia boonies to make out and maybe even hump. So it was around midnight and they was parked a ways down from the tower. Turned off the lights and climbed into the backseat of Darrell's Camaro and I think they'd maybe gotten to second base, he had his hand in her bra and he was squeezing her ginormous bazooms.

They heard a noise.

Darrell looked out the windshield while Lee Ann buttoned up her shirt real quick. It was pitch-black. Maybe a minute later they heard that sound again, across that field, near where those cannons stand. Like chains rattling. And Lee Ann was starting to get scared and then through the driver's window she saw two green lights, like lanterns, swinging over the field. They was a ways off.

She closed her eyes, hoping she imagined them. Opened them and saw they come closer.

Except for those two green lights, set close together, the entire Chickamauga Battlefield was pitch-black. Darrell zipped up his jeans and locked all of the doors and crawled back into the driver's seat, but Lee Ann stayed in the back. He flicked on the high beams, and all Lee Ann could see was a few feet ahead, the curb and a swirl of dead leaves. She was getting real scared now and so was Darrell and then they heard that sound again, like rattling chains. I'm talking big industrial chains, like the ones you see down at Ross's Landing, where the riverboats dock. They decided to get out of there and Darrell tried to turn the key in the ignition, but guess what?

The battery was dead.

Lee Ann looked up again. The green lights was much closer, just across the parking lot. She coulda sworn they was green cat eyes glowing in the dark. Darrell told her to get down, so she scrunched up on the floor underneath an old blanket. They waited like that for a while. She was about to wet her pants. All around them was silence. After about ten minutes he told her he was going to go for help and she was crying her eyes out. Said she was terrified something awful would happen to him.

She couldn't see his face on account that she was down on the floor underneath that blanket, but his voice was flat. He said the light was gone, no more noise of chains. Figured he'd hike along the highway, flag down a car going to Fort Oglethorpe, stop at the Gulf station, and be back with a mechanic, thirty, forty-five minutes tops. He told her to stay down and keep the doors locked, no matter what she heard. She better keep her head ducked, not look up, no matter what.

No matter what.

He got out of the Camaro and she reached up and locked the driver's door behind him and just for a second she saw he was trembling with fear. She dropped back onto the floorboard and buried herself beneath that blanket. Had to piss something fierce, had no idea how she was going to hold it for no goddamn forty-five minutes.

A few minutes later she heard them chains rattling, only it sounded like it was coming from just outside the car. Then she heard a sound like a ghost moaning. All a sudden the car was rocking from side to side and she kept her eyes scrunched closed even though she was scared shitless and crying . . . they was a crash and the whole back of the car lifted off the ground and then slammed back down. She was sure she was dead.

A while later the moaning stopped and the car stopped shaking and it was quiet. Lee Ann was tempted to open her eyes but then she thought about what Darrell had told her, the part about keeping her eyes shut. Kept hoping he'd come back with a mechanic and a tow truck and the whole goddamn Georgia highway patrol. Then she heard another noise—the chains—but this time there was this whish whish like someone was swinging those chains through the air. Was an enormous crash on the roof and the whole car shook like in an earthquake. Then was still.

Lee Ann was saying the Lord's Prayer when she heard a click click on the window. Opened her eyes even though she wasn't supposed to and they was bright flashing lights and two patrolmen was tapping on the glass on her side of the Camaro. She unlocked the door but they blocked her. Didn't want her to get out of the car, not just yet.

They was standing in a spot of light, in front of their patrol car, and they had the high beams on so she couldn't see a few inches past them.

Asked her name, address, what the hell happened. Seemed most inter-
ested in getting Darrell's name and telephone number of his parents.
Said they was gonna escort her to park headquarters in another patrol
car. Said whatever she did, she better not look back at that Camaro.

No matter what.

She wrapped herself in the blanket and slipped on her sandals. Got
out and they immediately turned her and walked her away fast, away
from Wilder Tower. She had to run to keep up. And then Lee Ann
became aware they was other officers moving in the dark, a bunch more,
saw dark silhouettes and glints of badges. Blue and red lights flashing
nearby, off behind the trees at the end of the field.

The very field where we're sitting now.

By the time they reached another car, parked maybe a hundred yards
away, she was smelling like piss. Wet herself while those patrolmen was
hustling her away. She looked back for a split second and saw the rear
end of the Camaro all smashed in, fenders and trunk crumpled like
tissue paper, blood streaked across the roof. This huge chain wrapped
several times around and Darrell's body strapped beneath it, face gray
and mouth open like this, dripping blood . . .

~~~

"That's bullshit," Tad said.

"What I heard," Craig said.

"Swear on a stack of Bibles?"

"Swear."

"Liar lying before God Almighty," Tad said.

He lunged across the blanket and hooked Craig in an elbow
vise, toppling Trudie's Fanta can and geysering fizz over her
baloney sandwich and a slick of wax paper. "Dang, watch out
for my Doritos!" Craig said.

"You gonna burn in hell with Charlie Manson and the queer-baits," Tad said.

"Didn't want that sandwich anyway," Trudie said.

We were sitting on a checked blanket rippled over a thatch of ragweed down the slope from Wilder Tower, deep inside the Chickamauga Battlefield. Several congregations had driven across the state line for the fireworks. The rangers had opened up the lower field for parking, sumac and creeping jenny flattened by tire treads and spinouts, hoods and fenders of Mustangs and Bonnevilles freckled with mosquitoes and a few early fireflies. Beyond the rows of cars, a sprawl of white oaks and loblolly pine.

A massive Civil War battle had seethed across this field, artillery fire clipping branches and igniting fires that had raged around the wounded Union and Confederate soldiers, searing their lungs and scorching some to death. Decades later, in the 1890s, a military park was platted, pebbled roads carved out of the riotous woods and monuments erected to show the battle's shifting lines along Snodgrass Hill and near the Brotherton cabin. The park's crown jewel, Wilder Tower, loomed near the southern boundary, set a mile back from the Fort Oglethorpe highway; a white-brick, Norman spire nearly a hundred feet tall, gouged with ornamental, paneless windows known as gun slots.

The congregations had spread out their picnics on a lawn of crabgrass, closer to the tower. The sun had set, but a liquid light hung on while the crowd waited. The Chattanooga Symphony had arranged their folding chairs in a crescent, violinists nuzzling their instruments while the brass section stood in full salute, playing "Yankee Doodle Dandy." I could see my parents' blanket, my father chewing on a drumstick, a splotch of grease on his T-shirt, while my sister slouched against the Igloo cooler, whispering into Lissy Sanders's cocked ear. She was probably telling Lissy she did not under any circumstances *like* Craig Allison or Mitch Fulghum, but maybe both of them were kinda, sorta cute. My mother pitched a carton of potato salad into a garbage bag. She was wearing a denim wrap skirt and a shirt with a blown-up facsimile of my father's photograph, a gag gift from their last anniversary. She'd recently dyed her hair the color of rust.

Last night, at family devotional, we'd heard a story as sinister as Green Eyes, except this one was true, as it came from the Bible. We'd gathered in my parents' bedroom. My sister and I had knelt on the floor. My mother had scooted the portable television into its corner, dialed down the volume on *Hart to Hart* but kept the show on, the atomized image of Stefanie Powers and Robert Wagner boarding a Learjet reflected in her reading glasses. She'd kicked off her flip-flops and was leaning against the bed, spraying lemon juice into my sister's blond hair, an ant trail of razor stubble conspicuous along her shins. "Damn those roots," she said. My father sat amid a mound of pillows, cross-legged and pashalike, asked us all to please turn in our Bibles to Revelation. He read aloud slowly, in a formal drawl, as he did most nights.

13:1 And I stood upon the sand of the sea, and saw a beast rise up out of the sea, having seven heads and ten horns, and upon his horns ten crowns, and upon his heads the name of blasphemy.

13:2 And the beast which I saw was like unto a leopard, and his feet were as the feet of a bear, and his mouth as the mouth of a lion: and the dragon gave him his power, and his seat, and great authority . . .

13:6 And he opened his mouth in blasphemy against God, to blaspheme his name, and his tabernacle, and them that dwell in heaven.

13:7 And it was given unto him to make war with the saints, and to overcome them: and power was given him over all kindreds, and tongues, and nations.

"That's scary," my sister said. "Kind of like *Halloween*."

"*Halloween*?" my mother said. "Really, Dollbaby? If I hear you snuck into the Eastgate theater . . ." She rapped my sister's thigh with the brush, an exclamation point.

"Nothing's as scary as you and Lissy trying to get Mitch or Craig to like you when they got eyeballs in their heads and can see you're both flat as a board," I said. My sister jabbed a bare foot into my ribs, tipped me against the television screen. *"Ow."*

"Pay attention to the Word of God, and don't blaspheme with your silliness," my father announced from his perch. He explained that this was a portrait of the Antichrist, and that the seven heads and ten horns each corresponded to something that was going on in the world right now this very second. "We believe that the ten horns refer to the ten nations that form the Common Market," my father said.

"Just sounds like a scary monster to me," my sister said.

"Are we supposed to think that?" I said. "What does Brother Virgil always say? *The Bible is the literal Word of God.*"

"Sugar, you ask too many questions," my mother said. "Guess fifteen-year-olds do that."

Ask too many questions? They'd put these interpretations out there for my benefit, for my sister's, for Craig Allison's and Trudie Parham's. Since kindergarten I'd learned from all of them—parents, pastors, elders, Sunday School teachers—a simple maxim: there are true stories and there are stories that are not true. A distinction that sliced the world cleanly, like a Ginsu knife. "What about the feet of the bear?"

My father clapped shut his King James. "Another time," he said, waving away my concern.

Now he was gnawing the drumstick's gristle. A gust bowled over the Wilder Tower. My mother dabbed his chin with a paper napkin, said something I couldn't hear.

⌒

Tad Swope said:

That ain't what I heard. I heard something different.

Here's the God-honest truth: first off, Green Eyes ain't some ghost. Don't look like no man. He's a monster, a devil-spawn from hell, lurks at night on the Chickamauga Battlefield.

Furthermore, I suspect Misti Dawn Cantrell is a figment of your imagination. Know some folks out at Rolling Hills, go swimming at that pool, and I can assure you they ain't no Cantrells out there. And if they ain't no Misti Dawn Cantrell, they ain't no Lee Ann and they ain't no Darrell.

But they's definitely a Green Eyes.

Anyways, here's what I heard:

Two dudes come out here to the battlefield to smoke pot. They parked up on Snodgrass Hill, the most deserted part. Pulled off the side of the road to roll their joints. They was starting to get high when they heard a noise. Not that loud but strange, like the howl of a wolf far off. They figured it was a coyote like the kind you see on the back roads out by the dam and over in Sequatchie County.

They heard it again, this time real close.

One of them dudes flicked the high beams on and off. He was sitting in the driver's seat. He rolled down his window and blew out smoke and called out if someone was shitting around he was going to kick their ass. He flicked on the high beams again and this time saw something run off, not more than fifty feet away. Something that disturbed the mosquitoes. A dark blur, taller than a man, with a hunchback and long, streaming hair. Dude swore he saw the gleam of a fang, a pair a green eyes, phosphorescent.

Them dudes was scared shitless and rolled up the windows and locked the doors but kept their joints lit in the ashtray. They drove back toward the park entrance. After a minute or two, they calmed down and started laughing. They was seeing things. Must be some damn good pot. They turned back and drove up here to Wilder Tower, where it's deserted but feels less deserted than Snodgrass Hill, at least they's a parking lot, some open fields so you could see Green Eyes were he to come after you.

They parked and rolled a couple more joints, high as kites. They was laughing and telling each other about their favorite horror movies, The Exorcist and Halloween, and then they heard that sound again from over by the tower. They looked up.

Wilder Tower was all locked up and dark inside, but they saw a green light at the top, on the observation deck, that snuffed out. Then nothing.

They wasn't scared no more, maybe 'cause they was so high. They got out of the car and walked to the tower. That one dude who was driving dared the other one to sneak in—he was a real skinny dude, shimmied his way up the bottom of the drainpipe and then made it to the first gun slot, maybe fifteen feet off the ground. He was so skinny he slipped in and disappeared.

A few minutes later his friend heard him shouting, "I made it, I made it," and then that wolf howl, only it was a thousand times louder *and the friend let out the most bloodcurdling scream. That dude was pissing his pants but was frozen in fear. He heard his friend screaming all the way down the stairs of Wilder Tower and saw him jump out of the gun slot and then fall to the ground and crack open his skull, blood and brains oozing out . . .*

⁓

"Blood and brains oozing out," Craig echoed. "That's a good one."

"Do y'all believe in Green Eyes?" I said.

"Oh, sure," Tad said. "Like the Bell Witch." As Tennesseans, we'd all learned in school the legend of the harpy who had tortured the prominent Bell family at their farm near Nashville, long before the Civil War. She'd placed a hex on John Bell, the garrulous patriarch, driving him to lunacy.

"Witches and ghosts and monsters," I said. "Lordy."

"We need to clean up," Trudie said. She stood, short and muscular in her tank top, arms bulged at the elbows, dark hair clipped close to her scalp. She furled the edge of the blanket into a scroll, forcing us to stand as well. Behind her I could see a border of woods twenty yards away, a chink within a hedge of blackberry bushes. Craig let his knees buckle and his shoulders slope, mimicking a chimpanzee.

"Fireworks won't start for a while," Tad said. "Got to get good and dark."

"Let's explore," I said.

Trudie noosed the blanket around her neck. "Where?" she said.

I pointed toward the blackberry hedge. "Looks like a trail."

"Probably goes off to some monument," Craig said.

"We need permission," Trudie said, as always our voice of

conscience. I hoped she'd prevail, but Tad was already striding through the tall grass. He called back to us. "He's right: a trail. Watch out for them stickers." He held the briars back like the flap of a tarp.

"Cool," I said.

"Are you sure about this?" Trudie said. "The fireworks."

"Go on," Tad said. "Still a while before that."

The trail stuttered through dogwoods and kudzu bramble, foliage that stretched to the Fort Oglethorpe highway. In minutes we reached a clearing, a trio of plaques that marked the Confederate positions, where Johnson and Hindman and Preston had fought. Raised metal lettering fringed with Queen Anne's lace and a hive of yellow jackets. A silence prowled the heart of the woods. The light drained away, leaving the char of evening and a stifling heat. I heard a crack of twigs and pine needles behind me.

"Just a damn lizard, is all," Craig said.

I was breathing faster. Trudie leaned her butt against the nearest plaque, swatted the yellow jackets away. "Did y'all see *Halloween*?" she said.

"Not allowed," I said.

"Same here."

"I liked that creepy music," Tad said. "*Do-do-do-do-do-do-do-do* . . ."

"Kyle took me to see *The Texas Chainsaw Massacre*," Craig said.

It had grown darker. I remembered what my sister had said last night: *That's scary.* After we'd finished family devotional, I'd bounded down the stairs into my bedroom, tunneled beneath the sheets with my Bible and flashlight. I needed consolation—something about the beast with seven heads and ten horns had aroused a titillating fear. I heard a creak over-head, my father's footfalls as he ambled from room to room, killing the lights.

From Bible Drill I recalled another story riddled with dread and phantasms, the Witch of Endor from I Samuel, in the Old Testament. Waging a civil war against the upstart David, King Saul had sought out the services of a spiritualist, a woman whose profession he'd criminalized by regal fiat. In the village of Endor, near the battlefield, she conducted her illicit business under cloak of night. I found the chapter. The flashlight glim-mered orange beneath the quilt.

28:8 And Saul disguised himself, and put on other raiment, and he went, and two men with him, and they came to the woman by night: and he said, I pray thee, divine unto me by the familiar spirit, and bring me him up, whom I shall name unto thee . . .

28:11 Then said the woman, Whom shall I bring up unto thee? And he said, Bring me up Samuel.

28:12 And when the woman saw Samuel, she cried with a loud voice: and the woman spake to Saul, saying, Why hast thou de-ceived me? for thou art Saul.

28:13 And the king said unto her, Be not afraid: for what sawest thou? And the woman said unto Saul, I saw gods ascending out of the earth.

28:14 And he said unto her, What form is he of? And she said, An old man cometh up; and he is covered with a mantle. And Saul perceived that it was Samuel, and he stooped with his face to the ground, and bowed himself.

28:15 And Samuel said to Saul, Why hast thou disquieted me, to bring me up?

The answer was obvious to me: Saul had tricked the witch into conjuring Samuel, punching a hole into a fog of afterlife to suck the old prophet back, all to hear a tale of what would be. Stories, spoken rather than written, acts of sorcery and subterfuge, chanted around bonfires and in tents, muttered in fields removed from the congress of human affairs. Stories, fractured and horrific, sacred and profane, true and not true. *Why hast thou disquieted me, to bring me up?* The witch had shrieked, peering clairvoyantly into the agony of the following day, when Saul would impale himself on his own sword.

Stories, strung like beads along an abacus, parsed into rhythms, spliced by images, hinting at something.

Something feral stalking the darkening woods.

Trudie Parham said:

I heard something else, something completely different. Green Eyes ain't no man. Green Eyes is a woman.

After the battle of Chickamauga, all the Rebel dead lay scattered: skulls busted in, arm stumps, putrid flesh. There was no time to bury the dead. The bodies just lay out here and got bloated. That night some wagons come in with these women in their bonnets and gowns and gloves, dressed up like they was going to church. And they walked among the bodies, looking for their husband or fiancé or sweetheart. And most of them found their dead men, and a wailing went up into the darkness.

But one woman didn't find her sweetheart. I don't know what her name was, but she was the most elegant of all, all done up in a silk hoop skirt with petticoats underneath and two bright green eyes in a pale face full of tears and grief.

She walked along gracefully with her parasol, calling his name. Don't know what his name was, either, but she called and called and there was no answer. At times she kicked over some dead, rotting body and screamed, but not because it was her sweetheart, because it was some half-decayed, putrid body. All night she searched and searched, disappeared like dew when the sun rose, nothing left of her but a faint cry. And each night all these years since, when night descends over the Chickamauga Battlefield and the Wilder Tower, she's back searching for him. You can see her green eyes and the out-line of her dress and bonnet, swinging her parasol and crying tears of grief.

"Complete and total horseshit," Craig said.

"You would know," Tad said.

"Y'all cut it out," Trudie said. "Look how dark it's got."

She reeled forward on the balls of her sneakers, tugged at the hem of her T-shirt to cool her waist, her armpits oily stains. She scratched her crotch absently, like one of the guys. The yellow jackets had faded into a darkness that was folding itself among the loblolly pines.

A rattle in the brush, around the plaques.

"We're disturbing the sleep of the dead," Craig said.

"Shut the hell up," Tad said.

"More lizards, I guess," I said. "Bet nobody's got a flashlight."

"We should head back," Trudie said. "Time for the fireworks."

In the subtracting visibility, Craig led the way down the

trail, the back of his head a pale wink. I heard a whistle like a
bottle rocket and glanced up, expecting to see bursts of gold
and blue. The symphony had ceased its playing, but evidently
the fireworks hadn't begun.

We came to a gully cut into a seam of orange soil and fes-
tooned with leaves. A fallen dogwood bridged the gulley, but
Tad tested it with his foot, said it wouldn't hold our weight,
so we scrambled down and hauled ourselves up the other side,
using a white oak's exposed taproot as a ladder. Trudie wiped
her hands on her shorts. She stank of oniony sweat. "Need a
shower," she said. Around us the leaves rustled and made us
think of copperheads and water moccasins. "Over that way,"
I said. We ducked beneath an arch of briars and stumbled into
the clearing with the three plaques.

"What the hell?" Craig said.

"How did we end up back here?" Trudie said.

Tad retrieved a book of matches from his pocket and struck
one to squint into the night. Still no fireworks to orient us.

In the brush to our left, a sigh of dead leaves. An owl's
screech.

A *pop-pop-pop* of indeterminate origin, off to our right.

The silhouette of a tall figure over there, antler branches, a
glimpse of a bloodred robe.

"Holy shit," Craig said.

"I'm outta here," Trudie said, kicking her way through a
thicket, hacking her own trail.

"Some crazy shit," Tad said, dodging the low boughs.

"Just keep moving," I said. "No way to screw this up."

"Shut up, fucker," Craig said.

"You ain't helping none," Tad said.

A scuttle among the trees just ahead, a moan, a chain rattle. Nausea garroting my throat. Trudie plunged forward, into the clearing with the three plaques, Johnson and Hindman and Preston.

"How? How?" she said.

"Better pray to Jesus," Craig said.

"This sucks shit," Tad said, chopping his hand, karate-style, toward the first path.

We'd gone maybe twenty feet from the plaques when Craig screamed. I glanced over my shoulder: he'd collapsed onto the path and was thrashing like a mauled deer.

"Run, you fuckers!" Tad shouted.

"Tripped," Craig called out. "Shit." He pillowed his shin against his chest as Trudie grappled beneath his arms, easing him up to a shaky stance. "Ow, ow, fuck," he said. Tad trotted over. "A scrape is all," he said.

I heard the sound of a struck match.

A swish of leaves, a hiss of wind.

A *thwack thwack* like the crack of a belt.

"Green Eyes!" Tad yelled.

"The Bell Witch!" Trudie yelled.

"The Witch of Endor!" I yelled.

"God bless America!" Craig said, limping forward.

A *thwack thwack* from just behind, between us and the plaques.

Tad stabbed his body through a drapery of kudzu. I felt sticky vines around me and then dove into high grass, falling onto Trudie, kneeing her in the thigh.

"Damn you," she cursed.

We'd torn ourselves from the woods and now slumped on our sides, staring ahead. The Wilder Tower was soaked in spot-light, its profile metallic, a portal to that other world, hidden among the woods. The various congregations had clumped near the orchestra as they struck up "My Country 'Tis of Thee." A whistle and boom as rockets shot high and blossomed, chrysanthemums that cascaded into a silver tinsel, sparking *oh my*s and *holy cow*s.

The woods receded, beaching us along an arc of shadowed field. More fireworks and cheers, a crescendo of cymbals. We huddled for another moment, panting, stick figures in a child's diorama, each brash young life a box brimming with worries, desires, trinkets–a minié ball plucked from a battlefield, a Bible with yellowed pages, a condom still in its wrapper—all diminished beneath a leaden sky, a flurry of Roman candles, two orbs glowing green and knowing above the crowd.

II

SEARCHING
FOR VASHA

Face facts: you're in a pickle. A quandary, a dilemma.

On the one hand, you need to ace this upcoming English exam. Your college acceptances may well hinge on a dazzling final. You're weaker on poetry and grammar, so you need to make up any lost ground with vocabulary and Modern American Drama. Compensate, counteract, offset.

On the other hand, your applications reveal other aspects of your personality. Cross-country team, school newspaper writer, student representative to United Way. A key player in your youth group. College admissions committees weigh these extracurricular activities appropriately. Judiciously, aptly. Could tip the scale in your favor.

On the other hand, you really *must* slam-dunk the English final. Last year's European History grade blots your transcript like dribbled ink. You'd crammed on Robespierre, all those stoic Versailles aristocrats mounting the scaffold in the Place de la Concorde; boned up on the covert alliances exposed by the assassination of the archduke in Sarajevo. You'd assumed the essay question—60 percent of your grade—wouldn't concern something as recent as World War II, so you were caught off guard when asked to analyze the decline of the Weimar Republic, Hitler's consolidation of power, Kristallnacht.

History's never been your forte, your métier, and no wonder. Except for a Civil War battle over a century ago, history just doesn't happen in Chattanooga, it happens elsewhere. Here people get up each morning, work their jobs, attend high school football games on Friday nights, church services on Sunday mornings and evenings. They swing through the drive-in lanes at McDonald's or Captain D's on Brainerd Road, order a fillet of fish sandwich, large fries, extra ketchup. The frame of life in this place.

In a panic you put down your pencil and asked yourself: the Anschluss, what's that? The ghettos of Warsaw and Lodz? That B chipped away at your chances. Undermined, eroded.

On the other hand, colleges will excuse less than stellar grades if you demonstrate that you're a vital member of a community. A leader: essential, exemplary. If you're elected Youth Week Pastor, for instance, what university could resist?

"Comrade."

My friend Trudie Parham interrupted my internal debate when she found me hunched over the scene of John Proctor in jail, suffering the burden of apostasy as he awaits the hangman's noose. With graduation just weeks away, I'd skipped Wednesday prayer meeting to read through my notes on *A Streetcar Named Desire* and *The Crucible,* paperbacks assigned in English class and my guilty pleasures. I'd tucked myself behind the Doric colonnade outside the church nursery, fretting that Mr. Sanders or Mr. Welch might discover me with my contraband literature. Since I'd entered the Youth Department back in seventh grade, the elders had formed a loose confederacy to groom me for the coveted position of Youth Week Pastor, the pinnacle of accomplishment for Baptist boys. Lately, though, word was circulating that my attention had fallen off in Sunday School, that I'd been seduced by books I could do without, like the ones confiscated at last year's *Catcher in the Rye* protest.

I have always depended on the kindness of strangers. At the age of eighteen, I could bull my way through a five-pager: Stanley Kowalski as the agent of tragedy, rebirth metaphors in *Ariel.* Turn in the paper, get the A. But in truth something deeper was pulling me, like an undertow. These sentences and enjambments had begun to resonate more than all those verses I'd scanned, right up to the book of Lamentations, where four years ago I'd dropped my diligent, nightly Bible readings.

Trudie had been shooting basketballs in the gym, so her face was ruddy, a trickle of sweat ran along her headband. "I'm here to liberate you, my brother," she said as she slumped next to me. "My mom got the keys to the church van, and I'm supposed to round up the youth."

"Liberate, emancipate, enfranchise," I said.

"What are you, a thesaurus?" She punched my shoulder. "You need a study break."

"Arby's!" I said.

"Burger King," she voted.

I'd known Trudie since we'd been in the same kindergarten and Sunday School classes. Even at the age of five we'd made a peculiar pair: the slight bookworm who'd already learned to read, with an owlish stare and manner to match; and the stocky tomboy who shunned dresses and tea sets and Easy-Bake ovens and could throw a ball farther than anyone her age. This bond had strengthened into our teenage years, despite the fact that we attended different high schools, pursued different interests. She was a three-sport varsity letterwoman while I'd had to sit out my junior season of cross-country because of a stress fracture; she excelled in calculus and chemistry while I preferred Spanish and English. We'd always help each other out, though. During worship service, we'd sit together near the back of the sanctuary, our Trapper Keepers fanned across a pew, working through quadratic equations or laughing silently at the melodrama in *Jane Eyre,* scribbling scornful notes on the back of the bulletin: "O Mr. Rochester, let me recline on thou!"

One of Trudie's talents endeared her to me: by third grade I'd discovered she had a beautiful singing voice, and could harmonize instinctively. In Sunday School we'd composed a simple song to help us remember the sixty-six books of the Bible in proper order: *Genesis, Exodus, Leviticus, Numbers, Deut-Deut-Deuteronomy, Joshua, Judges* . . .

Ten minutes later we were climbing into the van: Mandy Welch; Craig Allison; Mitch Fulghum; Tad Swope, who at six two needed the backseat to himself; the pious, insufferable Dannette Parsons; Trudie and me. Petite, with a bob of salt-and-pepper hair, Mrs. Parham slipped into the driver's bucket seat, snapped her seat belt, looked back over her shoulder. She announced in her preternaturally cheerful voice, "We're going to the St. Barnabas Home. Brother Odie gave me permission to take y'all over there and be back by the time prayer meeting lets out."

She shifted the gear to drive. "Part of our outreach to the elderly and homebound."

I was sitting in the passenger seat beside her, and glanced warily around the van. With the exception of Dannette, who wore floor-length floral-print dresses and yearned to be a missionary, the other kids seemed disappointed. We'd all been hoping for a run to McDonald's or Pizza Hut, since we'd avoided the meal served in the Fellowship Hall, sniggeringly referred to as "Chicken Barfizzini."

"I thought we was going to Arby's," Craig said. From the backseat, Tad said, "I been thinking about a Quarter Pounder all day."

Mrs. Parham promised that, if we finished in time, we could swing by one of those drive-through windows on Brainerd Road. Privately I, too, felt deceived, but tossed off a couple of isn't-it-wonderful-we-can-do-this sentiments certain to alienate my peers. I was in a difficult position. The election for Youth Week Pastor was slated for next month, and I wasn't exactly a shoo-in, so a little ingratiating with influential figures like Mrs. Parham made political sense. I needed one more accolade to propel me forward, one final thread to tie up my childhood, move on.

After parking in the St. Barnabas lot, we ambled through the glass doors and halted in the lobby. Mrs. Parham instructed us to choose partners and meet back in an hour. We were here to mingle with the residents, spread God's love. I hooked my arm in Trudie's, and we meandered through the room. A television set blinked on and off in the corner; an aide twiddled the dial for better reception. One man, scarecrow-grizzled and wearing soiled pajamas, was lashed to his chair. He pawed the air, fighting his restraints, tongue lolling from his mouth. A covey of older women, plump and whiskered, sat sedately on a couch, bathrobes cinched around their waists, faces bent over their crochet.

"Come say hello to Mrs. Bridges," Mrs. Parham called out to us. We paused in front of an obese woman sunk down in a wheelchair like a potted plant, her eyes watery and vague, a single brown tooth. As Mrs. Parham clasped Mrs. Bridges's limp hand, Trudie and I sang "Redeemed, How I Love to Proclaim It!" a cappella, her precise alto masking the lapses in my baritone, both of us picking up the tempo as we segued into the third verse:

> *Redeemed and so happy in Jesus*
> *No language my rapture can tell;*
> *I know that the light of His presence*
> *With me doth continually dwell.*

Mrs. Bridges nodded, faintly aware of the hymn. As Mrs. Parham leaned forward to the woman's ear, speaking in a too-loud voice about how we were from the Baptist church and just wanted to share God's love with her, Trudie and I eased away and into the building's residential wing, retreating from the senility on display in the lobby.

Through an open door, we noticed a fragile, diminutive woman alone in her room, clutching a walker. She lifted her chin to appraise us. She wore a tailored black dress and a gold Star of David pendant. Her white hair feathered around her wrinkled face; her lidded brown eyes conveyed she was all there. Her straight-on gaze seemed an invitation. Trudie and I came to her side and said our names, and she released one hand from the walker to touch our shoulders. "Could you help me?" she said, her voice edged with an accent—European, I guessed, although it didn't sound French or Spanish. "I'm not sure where the nurse got to." We scanned the room: a low single bed, neatly made, with a patchwork quilt turned down;

a glass-topped dresser with a couple of framed photographs; a TV dinner table with a crystal goblet of ice water; and in the corner, a floor lamp and a rocker with burgundy velvet cushions. We escorted her to the rocker, one step at a time, holding her by the elbows as she lowered herself.

"Thank you so much for your kindness," she said. "I am Mrs. Stein." She offered a steady hand, skin veined and translucent. "You are such nice young people." *Yunk peebul.*

"You're very, very welcome," I said, cutting a glance at my friend. "Very welcome," Trudie echoed.

Mrs. Stein smiled as though we'd arrived punctually for an appointment. "Those are nice pictures," Trudie said, pointing to the photographs on the dresser—a faded sepia portrait of a young woman with a slender, sculpted neck, a daub of shadow along the clavicle, the gleam of a part in her dark hair; a couple of glossy snapshots from a later period, perhaps the 1950s, a quartet of middle-aged women reclining against a Chevrolet sedan, mouths ovaled with laughter, gray, frizzy hair wreathing their faces. One held a Coke bottle.

Mrs. Stein nodded. "Yes, those were my sister and cousins, taken at the beach at Atlantic City, behind the frankfurter stand." *Vhrankvurter.* "We used to parade up and down the boardwalk in our spring frocks. Another cousin, a boy, would roller-skate and whistle at the ladies. And that"—she arched her eyebrows at the portrait—"that ravishing girl was me, once upon a time."

That rahfishink gel, vonce upon a tem.

We couldn't think of anything pithy to say, so we sat Indian-style on the floor, a few inches from the rocker. "Are you comfortable?" Trudie said.

"Oh yes, very comfortable in my new chair," she said. "My

nephew brought it from Atlanta. Not a kid anymore, but he is still strong . . . incredibly strong."

I shied away from the premise of this visit. I could tell Mrs. Stein that we were from the Baptist church and we wanted to share Jesus' love with her, but I was fairly sure she could care less. "You are from Europe originally?" I said.

"Yes, yes, I have been many years in United States, but I was born in Europe, in Vasha."

"That was the name of your town?"

"My town, yes. Vasha, so beautiful." Her voice lilted into a tranquil singsong like I'd heard my mother's do when recalling her girlhood in rural Georgia, the cadence of the fabulist, but with Mrs. Stein this seemed genuine rather than affected, seductive rather than irritating. "So many years since I last stood in the market in Vasha, but *here*"—she touched a finger against her temple—"I see it every day."

"Tell us about Vasha," I said. The Old World rose behind her words as she conjured a prosperous town, bustling with guilds and open-air markets and artisans. Kiosks where she'd buy cheeses for her mother, perhaps some marzipan and a bottle of mineral water on the holidays. One man would sell books from a wheelbarrow. A woman would give piano lessons in her house overlooking the public gardens; in summer a scent of lilac would waft through an open window.

She described mountains off to the horizon, blue with distance; green fields all around the town, where the farmers worked. In Vasha the grand boulevard ran west from the main square, along a river, where bankers and business owners lived in opulent villas.

She paused, puzzling over a detail that seemed to trouble her. "There was a lake," she said, staring up at the ceiling.

For a long moment she was quiet. I could hear a chorus of "In Remembrance of Me" from the lobby, Dannette's assured soprano soaring above a throaty, off-key tenor.

"A lake?" I prompted.

Mrs. Stein smiled a crooked line, eyes limpid. "A perfect circle in the heart of Vasha. Clear water, not deep. You could see almost to the bottom. My sisters and I, we would row into the middle and sing songs and feed bits of challah to the geese. Rachel would bring her cello."

"So beautiful," Trudie said, swimming through a trance.

"A perfect circle, like a china plate or the face of a clock," Mrs. Stein said, rocking back and forth. "Such clear water you have never seen . . . you weren't allowed to bathe in it. There were always a few young men sneaking into the lake in the hot weather, against the rules."

She breathed lightly, a rumor of laughter, unclasped her hands. "A few young rascals." She wobbled to her feet. "Time for my medicine—past time." She smoothed down her dress, accepted the walker from Trudie, and steered her frail frame toward the open door. "Where did that nurse get to?"

Back in the van, as we pulled away from the Wendy's take-out window, I cradled my paper boat of French fries in my lap, casually asked Mrs. Parham when could we go back to St. Barnabas. She kept her eyes on the road as we merged into the westbound lane. "I think that's wonderful!" she said, tossing an admiring smile in my direction, the clearest indication I'd had yet that I'd found a crucial advocate in my electoral quest. I did a quick mental calculation: a little over a month until the vote on Youth Week Pastor. I'd lobby for at least two more nursing home visits, pad out that effort with an extracurricular push, tendering my services in the Fellowship Hall, busing tables, maybe assisting the custodian on his runs to the Dumpster. Plus, I'd volunteer to lead the group prayer in Sunday School for the next three weekends—*nobody* liked to do that. If Craig and Tad and the other guys mocked my shameless campaign, so be it. The machinations that I'd set into motion the week I was promoted to junior high school and officially entered the Youth Department would finally bear succulent fruit. I'd make history: my name would be engraved on the plaque housed in the glass case just outside the church offices, along with the softball tournament trophies and the parchment Deacon of the Year citations.

Fame, sweeter than honeycomb, finer than gold; yea, verily, a lamp unto my feet and a light unto my path. I would increase in wisdom and in stature and in favor with God and man. My legend would inspire long after I had begat my sons, and my sons had begat their sons, a brilliant example to pimpled Baptist boys from generation unto generation . . .

I ripped open a plastic packet, anointed a French fry with ketchup, and glanced back at Trudie. She was staring out the window, subdued, her eyes clouded and her round face shadowed. Vasha had burst to life on some elliptical plane, intersecting with the only axis she and I knew: Brainerd Road, with its fast-food restaurants and car dealerships, massed near the floodplain of Chickamauga Creek; the upper reaches, toward Missionary Ridge, with an Olan Mills studio and the Moda Tienda Salon; the beige-bricked B'nai Zion synagogue, where I'd once gone for the Hochman twins' bar mitzvah; and, most significantly, God's Mile, the cluster of Baptist and Methodist and Presbyterian and Episcopalian churches, each buying up vacant lots as part of a brewing expansionist war. Copernicus-like, Mrs. Stein had drifted into our tight, confined orbit and shattered our sense of the universe.

I knew Trudie would go back with me to Mrs. Stein's room. But when we arrived one evening two weeks later, Mrs. Stein was standing with her face to the wall, wearing a slack cotton gown and gripping her walker. We helped her to turn slowly. Her eyes were confused, distressed, her tongue thrust against her lower lip, lizard-like. There were scabs on her wrists, a bandage around her throat, like a necklace. She tried to speak, choked on the words.

"Mrs. Stein, Mrs. Stein," Trudie said, curving an arm around her waist. We could see a prominent hump along her spine, her shoulder blades pinioned awkwardly, like the wings of a trussed turkey.

"Mrs. Stein, can we do anything?" I said.

A nurse strode into the room, a heavy black woman in a white polyester uniform, a Red Cross pin on her collar. A look of recognition flickered across Mrs. Stein's face, receded. "I just stepped away to speak to the doctor on call," the nurse said. That phrase felt ominously formal: *speak to the doctor on call.* "Awfully nice for y'all to come and sing for us." She folded Mrs. Stein in a robust embrace, planted her fists on the walker, barring her from us. "Now, Mrs. Stein, the doctor's heading over right now with the new medicine. I called your nephew; he's coming, too." With a nod toward the door, she dismissed us. "Thanks again, I know Mrs. Stein appreciates it."

I withdrew to the doorway, alarmed by the scene. Trudie lingered behind, her body stiff, a no-surrender posture.

"Mrs. Stein," she said. "Vasha, Vasha, beautiful!"

The nurse leaned her full weight toward Trudie; a second or

two of hesitation, and she'd levered us into the hall. We could see Mrs. Stein behind her, half-crumpled onto the walker.

"Thank y'all for stopping by," the nurse said. "I bet Mrs. Bridges would love for y'all to sing 'Victory in Jesus.' She's parked in her usual spot in the lobby." Trudie peered past the nurse, her hands balled into fists, until the nurse shut the door.

The next time we visited St. Barnabas, two weeks later, just before I won the election in an unprecedented landslide, Trudie and I walked anxiously past Mrs. Stein's room. The door was ajar: the room was empty, smelling of bleach and disinfectant, the bed stripped of her quilt and sheeted with starched linen. The rocker was gone. Someone had put a blown-glass vase with a few carnations on the dresser, where the photographs had been.

On a Sunday evening in late April, I delivered the Youth Week sermon from the pulpit, twenty minutes of standard platitudes spiced with fiery populist zeal, how we all needed to find the spirit of that old-time religion again, recover true, authentic feeling. Because of the warm weather, the deacons had propped open the sanctuary's front doors, and from the dais I could see the quiet street outside, a mown yard, a dog chasing a Frisbee. My true, authentic feeling was elation: I'd brought my church life to a graceful conclusion.

Afterward, at the reception held in the Fellowship Hall, I found Trudie by the refreshments table with Dannette and Paige Huckabee, the minister of music's daughter, surveying the spread: Pepperidge Farm cookies and butter mints and a prodigious bowl of punch with scoops of lime sherbet. I caught them harmonizing a Journey tune, a tad sacrilegious, given the evening's context:

He's tearin' you apart, oh, every, every day
He's tearin' you apart, oh, girl, what can you say?

Trudie was dressed in a denim skirt and plaid blouse with a velvet blazer, a ribbon tie loose around the open collar. She looked uncomfortable but smiled when she saw me.

"Slap me some skin," she said.

Our palms kissed, and then we touched elbows and bumped our fists, our personal code.

"You done good, soul brother. Great sermon. Radical."

"Thanks, comrade."

She'd stepped back from the other girls, bent close to my ear, confidential.

"Got something to ask you."

"Shoot."

She pressed a creased paper into my hand. "I got to go to the bathroom," she said. "Read this while I'm gone."

She strode away, bowlegged, weaving between knots of congregants. Dannette and Paige were talking about college acceptances; both had scored scholarships to Baptist schools. Trudie had scribbled her request on the back of the Calendar of Concern, with its hospital lists and names of shut-ins.

Will you go with me to the Central Senior dance?

I slipped the note into my own pocket. I knew now that this plot twist had always been lurking behind our conjoined history, tangible through pauses in conversations, the empathetic looks we'd traded in Sunday School and Church Training, all the jokes we'd written down in the margins of our Bibles when we were supposed to be listening to Brother Virgil's sermons. I'd always hoped we'd reach graduation with our platonic rapport untainted.

I felt a punch on the shoulder, firm but off-center, tentative for her.

"So what do you think, soul brother?"

For the first time I threw my arms around her, held her tightly, smelling her perfume and her own musk beneath it. "Let's do it!" I said.

She pulled back clumsily, as though the moment hadn't unfolded quite as she'd expected. "You're cool with this?"

"Positively," I said. "I'll pick you up around seven."

Central's final dance wasn't a prom, so fortunately I wasn't required to do anything extravagant, like rent a tuxedo or buy a corsage for Trudie. I decided to wear chino pants and a candy-striped oxford shirt. Trudie chose function over form: a short-sleeved chiffon blouse and pleated pants, one of those trendy belts with gold buckles.

In the car en route to the dance, we made tense small talk, mindful of the we're-just-going-as-really-good-friends aura we'd contrived. It turned out that I had an excellent time. The gym was decorated with crepe paper and maroon and silver balloons, the school's colors, strung from steel rafters. A DJ worked the front table, between trellises of speakers, a medley of retro disco and FM radio staples and the occasional Lynyrd Skynyrd or Allman Brothers anthem thrown in, to mollify the brooding, leather-clad Harley gang in the corner.

By the third song, A Flock of Seagulls's "I Ran," I'd figured out that Trudie moved like a bag of flour; her compact body, so agile and dominant on the basketball court, listed and flailed as her center of gravity migrated from her chest to her waist to her hips. I took up my mission enthusiastically. "Here's how you do the Shag, comrade," I said, clasping her hands and guiding her through a quick tutorial. After ten clumsy minutes, she seemed to get it, despite an elbow connecting with my jaw. We shagged through the most inappropriate songs, like "Free Bird" and "Sweet Home Alabama" and "We're an American Band," shifting tempo only for the classic closing dance, "Stairway to Heaven," where we held back from an embrace, clenched arms like two mannequins.

As I left Trudie on the doorstep of her back porch, beneath the mosquito light, I gave her a chivalrous peck on the cheek. We did our handshake. I'd never felt closer to her. Some essential question had been answered that evening, some oblique tension resolved. Our paths would gently fork away. We could forge ahead into our futures, craft our own destinies, look back on our shared childhoods with affection and nostalgia, when we even thought about them at all.

We couldn't have realized then, of course, that Mrs. Stein might have other, opposing ideas.

On the first anniversary of the terrorist attacks, I caught an express train from Brooklyn to the Upper West Side, changing to a local at Columbus Circle, planning to meet my wife at the office of her ob-gyn for an after-hours Lamaze class. I had no idea where I was going, and wondered vaguely if this meant I was unsuited for fatherhood, just a few weeks away. I disembarked at West Seventy-second Street and Central Park West, climbed the stairs into a cool, pristine September evening. A jogger darted into the park. Along the drive, some in-line skaters inscribed an arc around a horse-drawn carriage.

All day the city had borne its somber mood stoically, out of respect to the families that had gathered for the commemoration in lower Manhattan. In my private way I had observed the occasion. That morning, as I'd puttered around the apartment, I'd kept the television on, listening to the coverage at the World Trade Center site, the bagpipes' mournful airs and the recitation of the names of the victims. Although I hadn't personally known anyone in either tower, I still felt numb when contemplating the magnitude of loss, reminding me of other, exponentially greater atrocities.

Here, uptown, people nodded politely as they brushed past. Some stores had already shuttered. A solitary taxi bleated its horn. I turned the corner, headed toward Columbus Avenue, studying the façades for the address. Had I written it down correctly? This block was a row of anonymous office buildings, faceless awnings. I tried one door, but it belonged to a shipping company; another was the tinted door of a podiatry group now closed.

A few buildings down, someone buzzed me in. The occupant, a former manager of a dot-com that had gone bust, was packing her desk supplies into a cardboard box. She thought the ob-gyn office was next door. I thanked her and backed out and found myself on West Seventy-second Street again . . . *this* was bizarre, the street was quiet and virtually deserted, as though folks on the Upper West Side had made a communal decision to take the day off to reflect.

I glanced down at my watch: twenty minutes late, my wife hormonal and uncomfortable and likely pissed. We were just trying to move forward the way the city was moving forward, tentatively, green shoots in a field of ash. I gripped the handle of the next door down, expecting it to be locked. It swung ajar, into a darkened lobby.

Mrs. Stein stood there in her tailored black dress, frail and petite, her gaze alert and fixed on me.

A rahfishink gel, vonce upon a tem.

Beyond her, a cascade of light, particles distinct. I blinked and Mrs. Stein was gone, dissolved into radiance that sluiced through an open door. I stumbled into a conference room with chairs pushed back along the walls, a portable television set hooked up to a VCR, a half dozen pregnant women crouching on the carpeted floor, five of them reclining against their husbands' arms. One woman in the corner alone, tilted back forty-five degrees, cheeks flushed with anger.

Toying with my fixed notions, Mrs. Stein had withdrawn once more. One moment she'd been sitting cushioned in her burgundy rocker, spinning her story with consummate skill; the next her room had rearranged itself around her absence, her things carted away, leaving an antiseptic odor. After all this time I could still hear the burble of her consonants and vowels, as though she'd squeezed through a wormhole only to melt back into it, claiming a half-life the way the dead incarnate themselves in memory, again and again and again, each mole and chipped tooth and liver spot tactile, each black dress and sheer stocking and cashmere coat chosen to delight, captured the only way any of us are ever captured, in the body's details, eggplant hips, a whiskey laugh, flips on a trampoline. Words and images lopped off from the cinematic thread of history but enduring somehow, a high-definition video stored away in the lockbox of a child's mind. Your child's.

So many years since I last stood in the market in Vasha.

The Lamaze class ultimately didn't matter: in the delivery room, a fetal monitor picked up a fluttery heartbeat, necessitating a cesarean. In the following months, my wife and I wrestled with all the normal tests of parenthood, diaper rash and growth charts and 2:00 A.M. feedings, as well as a plethora of abnormal ones when our infant son was diagnosed with a neuromuscular disease. My old life sped up, slowed down, flowed away, replaced by a syncopated rhythm of hospital stays, respiratory treatments, nursing interviews, the arrival of healthy twins. Nights I'd crawl into bed, bone-tired, muttering a prayer for some supernatural intervention, an angel to guide me forward, a shaman to nourish me with incantations, magic.

An escape artist.

In New York the fantastic is always with you, tugging at your elbow, or pacing just ahead, a few yards down the avenue. On the subway, you'll see a pair of boys with their boom box, flipping like gymnasts the length of the car. You'll emerge into the ferment of Times Square, crowds milling around unicyclists and sidewalk games of three-card monte, a scantily clad cowboy picking a guitar. There's an acute feeling, too, of a darker, stranger world behind the protean street theater, invisible, but one that spawns its share of myths—crocodiles in sewers, mole people who roam the subterranean tracks under Penn Station and Grand Central, ghosts that haunt museums and grand hotels. The traces are everywhere: trapdoors flying open, windows banging shut, alley gates mysteriously unlocked. Even nature shifts shape. On one surreal occasion, as I rode the F train home from a night at the bars, I shivered as the train heaved itself along an elevated stretch of track—there, sitting astride the Williamsburgh Bank Building, a full pumpkin moon, apocalyptic, twice as large as I'd ever seen or would ever see again.

I fell into a funk one stressful afternoon, brought on by two sacks of dirty laundry, a broken toilet, a ziggurat of plates in the sink. Had I ordered my older son's nebulizer meds? Why hadn't that damned pharmacist called back? One twin wiped his nose on my corduroy pants. My wife stared blankly at me as I tried to make the case, in stammered fragments, why we needed a larger, more accommodating apartment. "I guess I'm just not getting through to you," I said.

Or had I forgotten something.

There was a lake.

That evening, after the boys were asleep and my wife was soaking in the bathtub, I booted up the laptop. First I tried Wikipedia, typed in "Vasha." A curt reply: "There is no title page called 'Vasha.' " I Googled a stream of links: a word from a lengthy title of a Polish film; a MySpace entry for a thirty-year-old Lothario in Vilnius; the personal website of a belly dancer down in Philadelphia; a planet in the imaginary Star Wars universe.

Perhaps Mrs. Stein's accent had obscured an inflection. More multiple spellings with umlauts and cedillas and circumflexes, a menagerie of exotic linguistic fauna. I tapped the Search key. Nothing.

Type, search, nothing. Type, search, nothing.

Had the Nazis razed Vasha, erased even a ghost of memory

that might have hung on after the war, in a street name, some fields along a river? What had happened in the lake? I imagined a cool night, the surface reflecting a wall of fire from the buildings along the quays. Perhaps the SS soldiers had rowed out to drop crates of valuables overboard, jewelry and Haggadahs and documents of families, evidence of the human business these people had transacted: marriages commenced beneath chuppahs, babies born wailing in four-poster beds; prayers offered reverentially in cloakrooms, words poured into the ear of a vigilant, paternal God . . .

Silly man. Here I was sitting on my couch in Brooklyn, my psychic antennae aimed speculatively into the past, and with all the technology at my fingertips I couldn't answer a straightforward question. *There was a lake.* I needed an ally in my search. I needed my comrade. Back at Google I typed "Trudie Parham," clicked the Search key.

And struck a lode: pediatric physical therapist, affiliated with a Southern university, specializing in treatment for children with neuromuscular diseases. From her celestial perch, Mrs. Stein must have orchestrated this kismet, pulled the strings just so.

Trudie and I hadn't spoken since early in our college years. Just after Mrs. Stein's death and the triumph of Youth Week, our respective paths, so entwined throughout childhood and adolescence, had rapidly diverged. She'd gone off to a liberal arts college in Missouri, where she'd shone as an athlete; I'd headed north to Virginia, where I'd buried myself in my classes and Student Council duties. There'd been a sudden glitch in our relationship, a short-circuiting of some vital neuron. We both had recognized this, and had moved on.

Such clear water you have never seen.

As my family slept in the back bedrooms, I composed an e-mail, jittery, saying key phrases out loud to make sure they scanned naturally.

To: Trudie.Parham@xxxxxx.edu
Fr: HCain@yyyyyy.com
Re: Searching for Vasha

Dear Trudie:

I know it's been about twenty-five years since we've been in touch (I'm not even sure I'm sending this to the correct e-mail address), but I've often thought about you. After college and graduate school I came to New York and have lived here ever since, first in Manhattan, and for the last six years in Brooklyn, opting for freelance work in the comfort of my apartment.

I got married almost twelve years ago. My wife, a native of Los Angeles, is an urban planner. We have three sons: Owen, just turned five, and the twins, Peter and Nathaniel, two and a half. Owen suffers from a genetic neuromuscular disease called spinal muscular atrophy, or SMA, which you may know from your line of work. He's cognitively normal but requires a tremendous amount of medical care as well as physical, occupational, and speech therapy and home instruction.

As a side project, I've been mulling something from our mutual past, which gives me the opportunity to shout out. Do you recall the trips our youth group used to make to St. Barnabas nursing home? You and I were seniors at the time, and once we dropped by the room of an older Jewish woman who told us about her early experiences in her hometown somewhere in Europe—the name "Vasha" sticks out in my memory. If you can recollect anything and would be willing to share, I'd be grateful.

Best wishes,
Hamilton Cain

I sucked down a shallow breath as though dragging off a cigarette, hit the send button, switched off the laptop, and padded down the hall, past the shadowed rooms where my children dreamed.

⌐⌐⌐

Amid the routine traffic of e-mail, I checked again and again: no response from Trudie. I attempted to rationalize my disappointment, leaven its severity—*what did you really expect, it's been decades, you're entirely different people with entirely different lives*—but the feeling still weighed me down. I'd assumed naïvely that, because she'd devoted her life to the care of children like my son, she'd answer. Toss a crumb of her own wisdom, help me to help him. Something, anything.

I gave her the benefit of the doubt, looked up the university's directory of e-mail addresses again. No problem there. A deeper Internet search revealed her recent presence on the West Coast, a panel in Seattle, a stint at a rehab hospital in California. Still, I couldn't use Google Earth to cross an X on a house in San Diego. I couldn't quite nail her down.

I recalled when we last saw Mrs. Stein, in the throes of a stroke, gagging on her own words. So much historical memory vaporized in an instant: Vasha, shimmering and elusive, forever a mirage. Now I was struggling to divine the mystery of a simple declarative sentence: *There was a lake.* Grappling with a sense that we were all poised on the rim of an abyss, howling mutely into a turbulent wind.

A prosperous town before the war. A bond as old as consciousness itself.

Type, search, nothing.

In a final bout of frustration, I wrote down the number of Trudie's department, picked up the phone, and pressed the area code and six digits of the number, hesitated before the last one, stunned by a thought. What was the point, anyway? Why this blind, foolish need to link my life with others, especially those who'd long ago disappeared behind a curtain?

For a while I held the receiver in my hand, disconsolate, standing in the middle of my bedroom as the phone's disconnect buzz droned on and on and on . . .

You know this feeling as you stand in the middle of your office, the phone dead in your outstretched hand. The building continues to shudder; the floor buckles. The alarms shriek down the hall, near the elevators. In the shock of the moment, you've reverted to that most primal human instinct: to call out to the people you love.

Your brother the police officer, hearing the breaking news on his radio.

Your wife at home, humming to your baby as she tapes his diaper shut.

Your father, dragging a rake across the yard.

Your grandmother in the nursing home, the one who favors black tailored dresses, whose old-country accent now rings in your head.

You fumble for your cell phone, but the signal has been severed. You dash from one side of the floor to the other, searching for a stairwell, some trapdoor of escape, but the fumes and flames block your flight. Already there's a dull pain in your chest.

You hurl a computer through a window, but that only siphons in fresh oxygen, drawing the inferno closer. It's worth it, though: the rush of clean wind pushes back the unspeakable heat, if only for a few seconds, creates a bubble cut loose from history long enough for you to take a deep breath.

From behind, you hear a din of coughing, colleagues slurring the Lord's Prayer, Kaddish. With your bare hand you knock out the remaining shards from the narrow window frame, brace yourself on either side, and lean forward, away from the ledge, suspended as from a gondola over the plaza a thousand feet below, watching as your burning comrades streak down like miniature meteors, all those lives radiating away from you.

As the smoke creeps back to shroud you, you glimpse a patch of sky overhead, just a few feet away. Such a clear sky you've never seen.

12

JAMBOREE

Three weeks after my mother's double mastectomy, she roused from her sickbed to announce she didn't care a fig what the doctors thought, she was taking me to college. At first she hobbled around the house, unsure of her balance; she'd halt in the kitchen or halfway down the stairs, bow her head in prayer. As her strength returned, she managed furtive trips to the drugstore and the bank, strapping on a pair of false latex breasts beneath a cotton jersey. She claimed that they felt almost natural, cool to the blistered cavity that now scarred her chest, a blessing in the sultry August heat. Each day she ventured farther. By the middle of the month, she achieved the dream that had percolated since that numbing, out-of-nowhere diagnosis: a Sunday morning at church, nibbling sausage balls and crullers in the Fellowship Hall, and then striding purposefully into the sanctuary for the service, recouping her usual post, left side, second pew back.

After the benediction, her friends and even a few enemies crowded her, patting her shoulder, telling her how well she looked. Even Mrs. Welch, renowned for her grudges, fawned

over her, that unpleasant business about the Women's Missionary Union's bake sale mysteriously forgotten. "Cholly looks like
a movie star!" she said loudly to Mrs. Sanders, her hand welded
to my mother's waist. "Barbara Stanwyck's *much* younger sister.
Never would have guessed she'd been through so much." My
mother preened in the light of celebrity. If she struggled with
any trepidation concerning the rubbery odor emanating from
her blouse, she never let on.

At the dinner table, she was jubilant. "I feel like a million
dollars, one hundred percent cured of that demon! Plus, I don't
have to haul those humongous things around—never again!"
With a flick of her wrist, she waved away the fear that had
stalked us all summer. That she'd been given a new lease, that
she'd circled back, hale if not exactly whole, to the normal
world, only stoked her desire to plunge back into the jangled
currents of life.

Which meant throwing herself into the opaque, increasingly
remote lives of her two teenagers.

I felt the approach of her will, dormant for the past weeks but
now bearing down like a locomotive, and glanced at my father
and sister to gauge their reactions. We'd all talked to God off
and on, but with diminishing gusto, each retreating down a
private alley, away from the spectacle of surgeons and catheters
and bedpans. My sister was spending most afternoons with her
boyfriend, her third in as many years, the one who'd given her
his class ring to wear. Her long stint as a tomboy had run its
course, the former football fan who insisted on Dallas Cow-
boys blankets and pillowcases vanquished by the debutante
with her head now tipped to one side like a model's, fine-cut
features and a flounce of blond hair. A rising senior, she would

be treading the same path as I had a year earlier, but she seemed more interested in fashion magazines than in college brochures and applications. This morning, in fact, she'd snuck copies of *Vogue* and *Glamour* into church. For weeks my father had been putting on weight: gravy biscuits for breakfast, Oreos for late-night snacks, deep-dish pies he'd bring home from Pizza Hut because my mother was too ill to cook. He'd try to offset the calories with salads for lunch but even then would bury the lettuce beneath a layer of bacon bits and ranch dressing.

"Stately, plump Buck Mulligan," I said aloud, although no one paid attention.

Since graduation I'd been laboring through *Ulysses* and had pushed through most of it, thanks to all those listless hours at the hospital, where I'd sat in the visitors' lounge, pale and gaunt and with a fresh spray of acne across my forehead, a creased paperback in my lap. Lately I'd taken to describing people and situations in Joycean terms, even though much of the novel exasperated me. Sometimes I'd flip back to the opening scene, where my narrative footing felt more secure, and read it again, Stephen Dedalus in the Martello Tower, quietly grieving his mother's death. *She was no more: the trembling skeleton of a twig burnt in the fire, an odour of rosewood and wetted ashes. She had saved him from being trampled under foot and had gone, scarcely having been.*

"An odour of rosewood and wetted ashes," I said.

"Don't mumble under your breath, Sugar," my mother said. "If you have something to say, well then, say it plain. Beginning to think those books are jinxing your brain." She scooted her chair back from the table, reached for a ballpoint pen and a legal pad and my father's bifocals. In the tense days while she was waiting to hear about the pathology report, she'd distracted herself by compiling a list of items I'd need for college: a window fan, a Lands' End backpack, an electric blanket for those frigid winter nights. "Better order you a scarf, too, some thermal socks."

She stood, frowning and perplexed. She had less than two weeks: the formal handing over of me to the adult world would occur just before Labor Day, and she wanted a proper send-off. She felt obligated to squeeze in a weekend trip to my grandparents' farm in South Georgia, as they'd been agitating to see her, their only child, back on recovery road. And there was the inconvenient matter of the Football Jamboree, scheduled for the same weekend as my departure.

"We'll go down to the farm on Friday, back on Sunday, find out how well I'll travel—maybe spread out a beach towel on the backseat in case I get carsick. Sugar, I told your grandparents you only answer to Big Man on Campus these days!"

My sister had stood, too, pivoting toward the den, hoping to seize the opportunity that had presented itself, now that my mother's attention had drifted away from her. "Sit back down, Dollbaby," my mother ordered, still staring at the legal pad, confident that her authority would once again rule the day. "We got things to discuss. We'll leave straight from the Jamboree, drive at least past Knoxville, and find a hotel. I just don't see another way. And we're *all* going, to support your brother, so don't even think about asking to stay with Lissy." She shot my sister a look that meant business. "Where did you put your pom-poms?"

My sister sank back into her chair, defeated. "They're in my closet," she said.

A slip of tongue inched across my mother's lip as she concentrated on the details. The meaning of life, she'd say, always lay in the details. "We'll need to swing by Loveman's for some eyeliner and maybe a little blush—not rouge, only tacky girls wear that, but a little blush will help you not look so washed out under the stadium lights."

She put down the pad and fixed her hands to her hips, impervious to my sister's mood, the false breasts askew beneath the fabric, a pulse of joy stiffening her spine—joy at the mere thought of having a future again, at the age of forty-eight, a *vita nuova*.

"What a way to launch your senior year. I sure wish I'd been a cheerleader."

My mother steered the station wagon along the lane, rutted as a cow path, as it meandered between burial plots. She parked beneath a cypress tree shawled with Spanish moss. We climbed out into the furnace of late August in South Georgia. A creek purled in bulrushes along the cemetery's fence. The tombstones gave off a marmoreal rebuke to the life that agitated beyond the gates.

Just days before the Jamboree, we'd driven south to the farm where my mother had been raised, deep in an agricultural belt of peanuts, sugar beets, and soybeans. As was our custom, my sister and I had spent the morning outdoors, inspecting the barns and silos, digging with a spade for arrowheads, accompanying my grandfather in the combine cab as he harvested his peanut crop. At noon we'd all convened in the front room for the midday meal, the air conditioner rattling in the window, cranked to full blast. My grandmother had brought out lima beans and okra and creamed corn, all artfully arranged on her floral china, along with a plate of buttermilk biscuits and a honey-glazed ham.

"Save room for dessert, y'all," she said, loosening her apron. "Marble cake and lemon pudding."

I was ferrying the leftovers back to the kitchen when I heard my mother propose a visit to the cemetery. She wanted to set a potted chrysanthemum on my brother's grave. My father had demurred, and my grandparents were busy with a new septic tank, so now just my mother, sister, and I wandered the headstones, searching for names that belonged to us, the Brands and the Owens and the Chandlers. Here and there my mother shaded in the contours of a life. "Mimi and Papa, I never liked that urn, but I guess they did that sort of thing back then ... Ah, yes, Aunt Georgia, quite the eccentric, that's where you get it, Sugar ... My cousin Debra, she had cerebral palsy, lived to her seventh birthday. Aunt Minnie said she died with a smile on her face."

She quieted as her internal radar locked on a plot that slanted toward the creek, a pelt of crabgrass and a single granite slab. My mother bent down, opened her hand to comb away a skein of weeds. "They'll get the Queen Anne's lace, but anything other than that, you're smack-dab out of luck," she said. My sister and I approached gingerly, looked down on what we'd left on our last trip, back before Easter: a chipped ceramic vase with a bouquet of plastic violets, a bunny face painted near the base, floppy ears and Betty Boop eyes. The summer storms had scoured the whiskers and snub nose.

"That vase didn't last six months," my mother said. She

pushed it aside and placed the potted flower on the slab, beneath the name and dates:

LANIER CAIN, JR.
AUGUST 3, 1961
AUGUST 4, 1961

I wondered how different all our lives would have been had he lived. As my older brother, he might have been a natural ally, taken my side in disputes with my sister or my mother. He would have handled the challenges of recent months with steely resolve and a casual charm, the flash of his grin bucking up the spirits of his family. I imagined his tone of voice soothing, his advice sage: *You should explore a bit during your first semester of college, a literature class balanced by Intro to Economics, or perhaps Astronomy—leave room for at least one class that appeals to you but about which you know absolutely, positively nothing. Maybe Environmental Science or Art History. Just do one thing for me, kiddo: enjoy yourself, okay? You'll never get this time back again.*

He had gone, scarcely having been.

My sister stood off to one side, curling a finger around a strand of blond hair. As children we had never discussed him, but we'd sensed how he haunted both of our parents. We understood that what had happened to him could happen to them as well . . . *would* happen, in time. Fearful, we'd creep down the hall to spy on my mother as she danced barefoot in the living room, her Lynn Anderson album spinning on the stereo's turntable. She'd wave to an invisible, admiring audience, her cha-cha-cha choreography flawless, *I beg your pardon, I never promised you a rose garden.*

En route back to the farm, I asked my mother about him. Through the windshield I could see a crop duster glide over fields of cotton bolls and shoulder-high corn. She adjusted the rearview mirror, tongue wetting her lips.

"He came too early, Sugar."

"What's too early?" I said.

"I was seven months along. He probably would have survived today. But you never know."

She'd seen him alive once, in an incubator the morning after he was born, a filigree of fine hair, capillaries flushed blue beneath reddened skin, a ventilator tube funneling pressurized oxygen in, out, in, out. For a while she'd watched the machine breathe for him before the nurse wheeled her back to her room. That was all.

"His lungs weren't finished," she said. "There was no way. We buried him in a blue navy sailor's suit. He looked like a dollbaby."

She guided the station wagon from the blacktop into my grandparents' yard, with its clapboard cottage and crepe myrtle bush and two men beneath the windbreak of pecan trees: my father whittling a knob of pine with a jackknife and my grandfather lipping his pipe. She braked and turned off the ignition.

"Remind me when we get back to Chattanooga to order that down coat from Eddie Bauer," she said. "They'll ship it directly to the dorm, won't they?"

An annual event, the Jamboree was held on a Friday evening, a preview to showcase the local football talent, a pair of teams scrimmaging for fifteen minutes until the next pair's turn, colored jerseys rotating in and out of a stadium built against the Chickamauga levee, mosquitoes swarming around the lights. We were planning to leave just as soon as my sister had fulfilled her responsibilities as the newly minted cocaptain.

When she emerged from my parents' station wagon in the Brainerd High School parking lot, you would never have guessed she'd spent the afternoon with her boyfriend at the golf course, firing up the links with her new 5 iron, returning home reeking of mown grass and late August perspiration. My mother had pounced on her as soon as she walked in the front door, escorting her to the bathroom. Now my sister wore a starched blouse and a tartan skirt, bobby socks and saddle oxfords, a tinge of blush across her nose and her hair smoothed back with barrettes. The pom-poms made her seem glamorous, nesting like a pair of enormous kiwis at her sides. She was sucking on a menthol cough drop that my mother had given her, to help her voice.

"You look lovely," my mother said to her. "But you're walking bowlegged, like a field hand. Be careful with your splits."

While my sister had been off playing golf, I'd packed the rest of my clothes for college, saving my books for last. In the car on the way back from Georgia, I'd reached the last pages of *Ulysses,* sucked down into the rich, mulchy Sargasso of Molly Bloom's monologue. I'd tucked the novel into my knapsack along with *The Moviegoer,* my favorite novel from the previous year, and *The Great Gatsby,* my favorite from the year before that. My father had wedged my suitcases and the steamer trunk into the station wagon's hutch, found a place for my tie rack in the glove compartment, although he'd had to clear out the Ritz wrappers first.

I knew the Jamboree's reputation for running behind schedule. *Please, please, not this time,* I thought, as I sat next to my parents in the bleachers across from the scoreboard. I only had to get through the Jamboree and then I was free. Released from the Baptists and their churlish manner, from the claustrophobia of family, an honorable discharge. So tantalizingly close, I could barely keep my butt pressed to the stadium cushion. The long shadow cast by my religious childhood spooled out across this field but no farther, cut off by the goalposts, the promise of a clean break, a football pitched elegantly into the palms of a quarterback.

He really believed it, too, this naïve, pious, fallen boy, frantic to pin down a faith that floated over and around him, a dirigible unmoored.

Two hours later my high school's football team surged onto the field. They'd won the coin toss and had chosen to receive the ball. Guys I'd play-wrestled with outside the cafeteria; friends who worked on the newspaper and yearbook staffs; acquaintances from the cafeteria, glee club, Junior Achievement. The cheerleaders stood poised near the fifty-yard line, chanted as the receivers sprinted past. My sister halted in midstep, watching the unfolding offensive play because it actually interested her, the ball's snap and the quarterback's ballet.

"Yes," she yelled as the running back scampered for a touchdown. "Yes, yes, yes!" She glanced in our direction, did a celebratory kick. I recognized the gesture for what it was: a valediction for a spindly girl who'd preferred gym shorts to dresses, played basketball with a boy's fervor, a girl who would cheat at Monopoly and Battleship rather than lose graciously to her brother. "Touchdown, yes!"

"Yes I said yes I will Yes," I said.

My mother rocked forward, borne on a wave of euphoria. She mouthed the cheerleaders' words: *Don't mess with the best 'cause the best don't mess, don't fool with the cool 'cause the cool don't fool!* She wouldn't have missed this evening for the world. The majorette thing hadn't worked out, but this was better: *every* girl wanted to be a cheerleader, but only a very few were elected. *She* certainly hadn't been this talented and popular, back in her small town in Georgia.

From this wellspring, her daughter's life would flow forward and deepen, a river with gleaming stones, teeming with jeweled fish. She'd been spared to see this happen. It was almost cruel, then, to watch my mother's expression as the fifteen minutes dwindled to seconds and then to zero. A game pistol cracked, and the referee rushed forward in his prison-striped uniform, sweating and bellowing "Time!"

With the Jamboree concluded, we hesitated in the parking lot, next to the bus that would carry the players back to the gym. My sister twirled her pom-poms as the boys pumped their fists in victory. Once the door accordioned shut, she exchanged embraces with the other cheerleaders, a halfhearted reprise of "All the Way Down the Field." My mother stood back, hands folded across her chest as if to ward off criticism of its imperfections, listening to this sorority adjourn until next Friday and in no way feeling excluded. My father pointed to his watch, signaling his impatience, a desire to get on the road.

Inside the station wagon, he asked if we could bow our heads. He prayed aloud, requesting safe travels and for the Lord to watch over me in this next phase of life. He let the engine idle for a moment, hands locked on the wheel in the ten o'clock–two o'clock positions.

"Stay close to the Lord," he said, staring straight ahead, voice gruff.

The moment embodied everything about us, sitting there in the station wagon, conducting our own private prayer meeting in the dusk. A family simple in its dimensions, clean in its symmetry—father, mother, brother, sister—and yet stained with an ineffable sorrow, all those stories we'd pass along to our children like genes, some flawed, some redemptive.

Amen.

As we traveled north, the miles punctuated by high beams and taillights, my sister radiated a glow, chatting in the backseat with my mother about how well the routines had come off, how she'd shouted herself hoarse with mantras of "Rock Steady" and "Give Me a *D*." Gradually she talked less and less and then yawned, chin drooping on a down pillow. She stirred only after we'd pulled into a Best Western around midnight, just shy of Abingdon. She shambled to the room and wilted onto a bed, still wearing her tartan skirt and saddle oxfords.

The front desk called early, before 5:00 A.M. I'd claimed first dibs on the bathroom and took my time with my shower and grooming, tugging on jeans and a polo shirt and tousling my hair, hoping to exude a collegiate air. By 8:00 A.M. we were all back in the station wagon, heading northeast on Interstate 81, past places whose names would serve as markers for the next four years: Christiansburg, Roanoke, Natural Bridge, and my favorite, Hungry Mother State Park. I glanced over my shoulder: my mother had folded her legs beneath her, a swami on a blanket, looking out the window and forcing a thin-lipped smile. My sister sat next to her, wan and hungover from the previous night's emotions, her eyes hidden behind Vuarnet sunglasses and hair snarled beneath a plastic clip. Diminished, she listened to her Walkman so as to avoid conversation, aware that she'd conceded the day to me.

Beyond Lexington the freeway wound through a series of ridges and ravines, pushing into the Shenandoah Valley. My father turned on the radio, found a country station he liked, up near Staunton, classic songs from Patsy Cline and Hank Williams. *I've got these little things, she's got you. Hear that lonesome whippoorwill.* The sun was high now, near its apex. Lulled by the car's motion and a banjo's twang, I nodded off.

⌒⌒○

I wake as the station wagon climbs a steep grade toward the crest of the Blue Ridge. Now we are moving through the bald gap. On either side the world falls away into terraces of maple and live oak, outcroppings of granite. We ride the earth's curve for a moment, the sky a roof of cerulean blue, bright as a fresco. Overhead, a hawk hovers on thermals rising from the valley. A column of smoke tethers to the horizon, a brush fire lost among the green haze of woodlands.

We descend toward a place I'll claim as mine, the first among many places, there among the gullies and hills. Stands of ash and hickory arch over the freeway, hedges of blackberry veil the outskirts of the town. As the Blue Ridge's eastern flank flattens out, I survey the notched outline of the receding mountains.

The lanes empty of cars and eighteen-wheelers. In the backseat my mother and sister have gone mute, rigid as statues.

I breathe deeply, from the diaphragm. The last moment

before my adult life begins. Alone, the station wagon traces the road's seam, its cargo caught between a tenuous present and what's come before, the cancer excised and the false dreams discarded.

Somewhere among the trees the town waits.

IN PROSPECT PARK

BROOKLYN, NEW YORK, AUGUST 2009

Dear Gabe,

How are you? What have your summer been like? I am having a great summer. Real warm here. Is it hot where you live? I am very happy you wrote to me. I want to be pen pals forever.

What is your room like? What kind of house do you live in? I live in a apartment with my own room. I live on the 3 floor. We want to move to California. I want to live in the trees and valleys. I like the country.

I want to visit Florida when I am old and go to the beach. I love sharks.

I hope I can write to you again because Robyn is who helps me write to you but she is leaving soon to marry Bram. I am going to try to write with my new nurse. I will be sad when Robyn leaves. She is a great friend and I love how she helps me write. I wish I could meet you soon. I will send you a picture of me.

I hope you are so good.

Love, Owen

"So we want to move to California?" my wife asks rhetorically, fondling Owen's letter in her slender hand. "Since when?"

Home early from work, she ballasts her hip against his bed, the one fashioned from bird's-eye maple by his physical therapist. She's imperious in a sheath dress. Light comes in lager waves through the double windows, dousing the dresser and bookcase, an array of clunky medical equipment. I feel a stickiness from the air conditioner's concertina sleeves. Down the hall, our four-year-old twins bicker over a toy train.

"I'll go," I say. "You can pick the place. Montecito, Carmel, Marin."

"This is adorable," she says, flicking the note in my direction. "But, hey, news flash: I'm not going back. Be like throwing in the towel."

She disappears into our bedroom to slip into a pair of shorts and a tank top. Squeals of distress from down the hall. She cracks the door an inch. I imagine her hands megaphoned around her mouth as she calls, "What's the magic word, boys? *Share.*"

Anchored by pillows, Owen nests in the dimple of an oversize velour beanbag, his feeding tube snaking over the crown, a cannula tight in his nostrils. His BiPAP ventilator pumps air in, out, in, out, a steady *whoosh-whoosh,* twenty-five breaths per minute. His hazel eyes are wide, watchful, his feet slack and turned inward at the ankles, a merboy's. For the past hour his nurse, Robyn, has crouched at his side, her forearm cradling his elbow, her reedy wrist melded to his slack one.

Last year his occupational therapist, Cathy, discovered that if you held his wrist at a particular angle, Owen could guide a felt-tip pen across a slate, summoning the tiniest fragment of motor neuron ability—about 1 percent of a healthy child's—to express himself. At first he wrote only nouns and verbs in block letters, but then simple thoughts molted into complete sentences, impressions rendered in a barbed, Germanic script. *Running is freedom. Happy you're here now. You are the reason I am good.* Eventually he perfected a kind of calligraphy, scrawled but stylish in its own way, *m*'s and *n*'s whale-humped, capital *S* and *F* curlicued like treble clefs. Cathy taught us all how to hold his wrist, with varying degrees of success.

Robyn seemed most skilled at following his lead. She'd sit with him for hours as he bore down on his slate, filling notebooks with questions and comments about sharks and space. *The great white shark swims in the ocean. How far is the nearest supernova?* She came up with the idea of a pen pal for Owen: a friend's seven-year-old son, down in Fort Myers, a boy rooted in a place, his life contoured by sunburn and hurricanes, sugared beaches and conch hunts, alligators waddling onto golf courses. Gabe's letters wandered from image to image, sloppily spelled, but Owen loved each word.

Florida, a place he longed to see, someday. He'd said so, in his letter.

As an infant, Owen had been hospitalized at Columbia Presbyterian for seven months. We'd struggled to determine a diagnosis and then to craft a protocol of care for him. Ellen and I had swapped shifts at his bedside, riding the subway back and forth from downtown Brooklyn to Washington Heights in Manhattan, an hour each way; despondent, dwindling to scarecrows. We'd whispered counsels with nurses at midnight;

we'd breathed the smells of camphor and disinfectant; we'd suffered migraines caused by fitful sleep on foldout couches. We'd put aside books and magazines to take up rubber catheters, humidifiers, Lilliputian probes taped around Owen's toe to measure his heart's *lub-dub, lub-dub.*

After his discharge, we'd structured our lives around his medical routines—an edifice jerry-rigged at first, since we didn't know anything. A plank here, a window frame there. We'd started over again, marshaling tools. We'd welcomed nurses and therapists. We did respiratory treatments every six hours, with frequent trips to the pharmacy. Owen had faced it all with guileless cheer, smiling at us from his crib (and later from his exquisite Shaker-style bed), staring stony-faced only when his brothers had arrived, two years later. He'd grown lean and long, hair rumpled like a mop.

Today I've caught up on chores, cleaning out closets, filling saggy cardboard boxes, twining together yellowed clippings from *The New York Times,* old alumni magazines, stacked them all by the front door, ready for the recycling bins. At the bottom of one box, I'd found Owen's X-rays from his initial hospitalization, over six years ago, the film aged to a spectral purple, his collapsed lung and contorted spine bathed in a chalky light, a window into the boy he once was. What had that first pulmonologist said? *An X-ray is a two-dimensional image, a snapshot in time, and gives us only a limited amount of information.* You won't learn the extent of what goes on inside this boy by just studying a snapshot in time, darkening like a memory. Now Owen was chronicling the comings and goings of nurses and therapists, the jokes his parents swapped, and the capers of his brothers, an astute observer of his world. *I live in a apartment with my own room.* I'd put the X-rays in a garbage bag, their purpose served.

The phone rings. I dash into the living room, leap over the twins as they scrap in a half nelson, pick up the receiver.

"Sugar!" Her drawl is fainter now, but still musical, consonants and vowels mashed like a gumbo, bayou-lush. "Y'all getting along okay?"

"Fine, Mother," I say. We make small talk: the muggy weather, my sister's children, an old church friend whose marriage had mysteriously dissolved.

"*Very* abrupt," she opines, a distinct *tut-tut* tone in her voice. "At least they didn't have kids."

"So what's the story?"

"Can't say I know. No one tells me anything."

"You must know something," I say.

A sigh of annoyance. "I really don't."

"C'mon."

"I. Do. Not. Know." She lets her voice trail off airily, mimicking Vivien Leigh's in *Gone With the Wind*. "You always were a difficult child. Well, been there and done that."

"Tell me tell me tell me," I say.

"*I do not know!*"

I picture her with the receiver tucked beneath her chin, mouth hardening, the old light of battle in her hazel eyes. I clear my throat. "Mother, when you say you don't know, that means . . . you know."

A guffaw of exasperation, sudden surrender. "All right," she says, "I'll tell you what I *heard*."

For a moment we gossip. She conjures ghosts from the past: some dead, some still alive, Brother Roy and Miss Eula and

Craig Allison and Mandy Welch, names seeping through the connection to barnacle themselves deep inside me. When I ask about a possible trip to New York, she demurs, blaming my father's fragile health. After a polite good-bye, I hang up, shaking my head.

The twins swerve past the coffee table, engaged in a giddy chase. I head back to Owen's room, where he's illustrating his letter with a decorative border, daisies and a pulsing, psychedelic sun.

From his side, Robyn glances up. "He wanted to draw a little," she says.

This is Owen, embarked on his quest for the beautiful and true. Many years ago, when my parents had delivered me to the laboratory of college, they'd assumed I'd humor myself for four years, Kierkegaard and Shakespeare and Dostoyevsky and Plath, field trips to the National Gallery to analyze canvases by Goya and Van Gogh. Four years, and no longer. They'd trusted the Lord would wean me of any humanist impulses, steer me back to the world that had reared me in its insular, painstaking morality. Values were values, after all: immutable, transmitted from generation to generation through hymns, sermons, ordinances like baptism and the Lord's Supper, Bible Drill, Youth Week. The work of the soul was the tribe's DNA.

That first semester I'd taken a seminar on Plato, jotted notes about Socrates' trial, *The unexamined life is not worth living.* From then I stared straight ahead, blinkered: literature and art history classes and then north to cosmopolitan New York, capital of poetry readings and liberal politics, African art exhibits and Bergman retrospectives; genteel Manhattan gallery openings, where glamorous women and debonair men sipped flutes of champagne and nibbled on bite-size canapés and charcuterie, pattering wittily about Roth and Frankenthaler and Sebald. The Baptists receded, distant steeples in a rearview mirror.

But there'd been moments that triggered a feeble response: the lump in the throat when hearing Handel's "Hallelujah Chorus," for instance, on NPR in a dark room late on Christmas Eve. In twenty-five years I hadn't boycotted services entirely. Once or maybe twice a year I'd scratch the ancient itch. I'd shower and shave on a Sunday morning and head off to a local church, Catholic or Presbyterian or Quaker, compile mental notes as though researching an anthropological thesis. But I wasn't immune to religious feeling. I'd still shiver at the lavish textures and half-sung Latin of a Catholic mass; I'd bask in the spiritual passion raying out from the canvases of Tiepolo and Fra Angelico at the Metropolitan Museum. And this feeling wasn't confined to Christianity. Once I'd gone with a friend to an ashram on the Upper West Side, unexpectedly lost myself in the mellifluous chanting. And on summer evenings before Owen was born, I'd unwind with a glass of pinot noir on my roof deck, listening to the call to prayers from the mosque on Atlantic Avenue, the muezzin's voice tremulous with suffused pain and longing for God.

And then the towers collapsed and Owen came; the universe fell into itself as a baby fought for his life in a wounded city. God withdrew into His black hole, bending space and time and memory. The mosaic of feeling shifted again, scattering into arcane patterns, no map to shepherd me forward.

Or maybe I was wrong.

The values had always been there. Sacrifice, Steadfastness, Redemption, Apocalypse, Magic. Still clinging to me like burrs, after all these years. Somehow I'd circled back, a homing pigeon navigating all kinds of weather, wind-tumbled, drawn by instinct to contemplate God. Or at least to contemplate those whose desire for God tints every conscious moment.

Real warm here. I like the country.

And now to his friend Gabe, Owen has confessed a dream: to go west, to his mother's state, like generations of Americans before him, to be whole among the trees and valleys, breathing deep the tang of chaparral, his lungs miraculously plumped out like his brothers', his soul stirred by magpies' jabber and the howl of a far-off coyote. His manifest destiny, free from tubes and catheters; his wheelchair abandoned along the way, its purpose fulfilled, like a Conestoga wagon.

He loves the country. He'd written it down. Its gorges and waterfalls, undulations of peaks and deserts, mile-wide rivers, sawgrass wind-winnowed. I see him clearly as he stands for the first time, smelling the Pacific's salt as he shucks off the husk of disease, feet bearing his weight, pink with new feeling. His spine straightens, limbs loosening their crabbed claws. His people—nurses, doctors, therapists, brothers, parents—gather behind him, their faces shining as he spraddles over the last dune to the ocean. He gains confidence with each stride.

Is this not a tribe's raison d'être? To love and succor its children, teach them its ways, bear them forward, toward the horizon?

But I could tell him something he doesn't know yet: noplace will make him whole. No tribe will be there for him, come hell or high water, disease or no disease. There is no transcendence: only its hologram, a dream that fizzles in a nebula-darkness.

I want to live in the trees and valleys.

He moves out of view, into a dazzle of light. Nothing can kill this boy's faith.

My wife steps back into the room, clipping her hair with a barrette. "I'm thinking burritos for dinner," she says. She weaves around me, smiles at Robyn, and bends to brush her lips against Owen's forehead. "Bubula." His eyelids flutter.

"Think I'll take a bike ride," I say. "Need some air."

"In this heat?" my wife says. "We'll be eating in an hour."

"I've been cooped up all day, feeling a little light-headed."

With her arm poised along the beanbag, she forms a pietà with her oldest son. Perhaps she senses that a reckoning is at hand. "All right," she says. She nods, unfolds a fine-boned hand: a rabbi's numinous gesture, a priest conferring absolution.

Two months past the solstice, a warm, beery light soaks Brooklyn as I angle my Cannondale through Prospect Park. Sycamores flake their bark, leprous. Just inside the gate, I arc around a child on a scooter, pedal past the lake speckled with swans and mallards. I feel the drag of humid air but push on, sealed off in my aerodynamic pocket, in the world but not of it.

I follow a winding trek past the Wollman Rink and the Audubon Center and the zoo, bisecting a spectrum of immigrant cultures. A troop of African drummers beats a tempo as a girl dances maniacally. Elderly Russian couples slump in folding chairs. Arab boys josh and shove near the boathouse. Orthodox Jewish women rocket past on Rollerblades, arms flailing, *schmatas* flying in a breeze. This is, after all, Brooklyn, its Babel of voices a symphonic answer to bigotries of all kinds, all these diasporas salved by their common mother in the harbor. *I lift my lamp beside the golden door.*

I wend my way along the East Drive, deeper into the park. A

grizzled man teeters on a dinged bike, a bag of zucchini looped over the handlebars. Pickup games of soccer in the Nethermead: Honduras versus El Salvador, Nigeria versus Senegal. A knot of Bangladeshi girls chatter in Bengali until one lapses into Brooklynese, *Oh-no-you-did-un-wid-your-hair.* I wonder how many of them hide, beneath brocaded silk, the scars of a tribe's yoke. Toward Battle Pass I shift gears, lean into a steep grade, winded, pumping hard. Joggers surge and lag at varying speeds, most of them in the proper counterclockwise direction, but I also dodge the occasional contrarian gliding against the flow: a bare-chested teenager midsprint, jet-black hair streaming back in a corona, smirk teasing his lips. *Him,* I think. *I know him.*

But I don't know, really.

Now I crest the hill. The park opens below me like a City of God. Damselflies flick and dart over the Long Meadow. Children erupt from playgrounds. Caribbean nannies spread out their blankets, rocking their strollers. Volleyball nets unfurl beneath the limbs of black cherries; a platoon of birders advances toward the Midwood, binoculars raised.

I remember the verse from near the end of Revelation: *And I saw a new heaven and a new earth: for the first heaven and the first earth were passed away.*

With each year the Baptist Boy I once was fades, his image now blurry, a ship steaming far out on the horizon. But as I negotiate the park's densely wooded interior, skidding along pitted trails, that past rushes back, Goya's hooded pilgrims on the road to San Isidro, the Sanderses and Drapers and Allisons. My parents and my sister leer and poke the heretic, demanding that I recant my chief apostasy: that I always saw myself as better.

"Sugar, I just can't come to New York anytime soon. You made a choice when you moved there. Now I'm making mine."

"I vote Republican because they stand for Christian values, Son."

"Stop talking over me, can't believe you'd disrespect your own sister, you call yourself a feminist?"

El sueño de la razón produce monstruos.

At the base of Lookout Hill, the park's highest summit, I dismount and walk the bike up the northern side. After ten minutes I reach the brow, prod the kickstand with my foot. There's a churr of cicadas, a buggy breeze. Perspiration glazes the hollow of my back.

As I peer into the distance—sun low in a bruised sky, Staten Island telescoped behind a palisade of apartment buildings— another prospect reveals itself. Owen: his desire to be an as- tronomer someday, floating beyond the cramped cell of his body. The facts that delight him: Jupiter is the largest planet, Saturn's the ringed one, comets swing inward from the Kuiper Belt to orbit the sun. His brothers, Nathaniel and Peter, speak a twins' language: *Bubba-catch* and *shoosh* and *teetob*. "What's a teetob?" I'd once asked. "Ees a leetle poo-poos," Nathaniel had said, squinting at me and pinching his thumb and forefinger together. The book of revelation, I know, belongs to the very young.

Or perhaps not. On my way home, I stumble upon an unex- pected vision: a beechnut tree jeweled with parrots, preening their plumage. I'd read somewhere they'd descended from a flock imported from Argentina forty years ago; the birds had escaped their cage while passing through the customs queue at Kennedy Airport, swooping over the city until they'd found roosts in Jamaica Bay's brackish marshes, church cornices, the green at Brooklyn College. They'd eventually brooded into a colony, the borough's most famous avian residents.

Now they sample seeds in their beaks, testing the shells. Their colors—fluorescent gray-greens, a glint of blue—echo the irises in the eyes of my three boys. I'm lost, as the old hymn would say . . .

Lost and then found.

Acknowledgments

For their insights, encouragement, and support: Konstantin Alexopoulos, Justina Batchelor, Paige Bowers, Lisa Drew, Henry Dunow, Sharon Dynak, Patricia R. Eisemann, Vida C. Goldstein, Paul Golob, Leigh Haber, David Long, Marcus Mabry, Tucker McCrady, Scott Moyers, Deirdre Mullane, Julie Z. Rosenberg, Jane Rosenman, Bettina Schrewe, Yishai Seidman, Anna Thompson, Emily Timberlake.

For their indelible contributions to this story: Lanier Cain; Charlotte Chandler Cain; Char-La Cain Fowler.

For a seemingly infinite number of kindnesses over the years: Charles Flowers and Jeff Kleinman.

For her singular midwifery skills: Kelly McMasters.

For his incisive early suggestions: Brett Valley.

For her virtuosity and faith: my editor, Suzanne O'Neill.

For her wise counsel and limitless good cheer: my agent, Betsy Lerner.

First and last: Ellen Goldstein.

ABOUT THE AUTHOR

Hamilton Cain was born in Orlando, Florida, and grew up in Chattanooga, Tennessee. He graduated with high distinction from the University of Virginia and received his master of arts in creative writing from Hollins University. A former book editor, he now writes for various publications and was a finalist for a 2006 National Magazine Award. He lives with his family in Brooklyn, New York.